SAM HOUSTON

AND

HIS REPUBLIC

1836   1845

By Charles Edwards Lester

Copano Bay Press
2019

Originally published in 1846 under the same title.

New material copyright 2019, Copano Bay Press

ISBN: 978-1-941324-36-3

CONTENTS

PUBLISHER'S NOTE

In the fall of 1846, Texas had been one of the United States for less than a year. The Mexican War was in full swing. The Liberty Bell had received the crack that would silence her peal forever. The Mormons were making tracks for Utah. The Donner party were beginning to feel peckish and the first biography of Sam Houston hit the shelves.

It was supposed that Houston would make a run for the highest office in the land in 1848. The publication of this book set political types and the media to salivating. It's not a good book, as biographies go. It doesn't say much of substance about Houston. It contains a fair amount of romanticized garbage and fictional dialogue, and is woefully lacking in its piecemeal recounting of how Texas came to be. It is essentially a eulogy of Sam Houston. The New York *Daily Herald* of May 1, 1855 described it as ably as anyone else:

> As a history, it is admirably adapted to electioneering purposes, full of the most dashing, romantic and fascinating adventures, battles, victories, incidents, privations, and heroic philosophy and endurance.

Mirabeau B. Lamar, writing to David G. Burnet, in March 1847, offered his take on the work. "You speak of a book called Houston and *his* republic," he writes. "*His* republic! That is true; for the country [literally] belongs to him and the people his slaves. I can regard Texas as very little more than Big Drunk's big Ranch..."

The gist of the book is this: Sam Houston was the creator and savior of Texas. Anyone who was *not* Houston played but a minor role or was plotting to foil his efforts at creating and/or saving Texas at any given point in the history. No other human, then living or dead, could have endured all the abuse he did or performed the feats that Houston performed. No one. The end.

What were General Houston's thoughts on the book? If I were a bettin' gal, I'd wager that he wasn't a fan. In a later edition of the book, the author, Charles Edwards Lester, claimed that he had unfettered access to the official papers of the Republic of Texas, as well as to Houston, Rusk, etc., while writing. In that same 1883 edition, Lester claimed that he wrote the entire book in three months in Houston's D. C. hotel room at the onset of his senatorial debut. If he truly had access to those resources—if the final product is any indication—Lester didn't pay them any mind. The book lacks dates, sources and anything resembling specificity. Letters republished here described as "private" actually appeared in major newspapers of the day. If Houston had an opinion of it, he was mum on the subject. I can find no record of him embracing or refuting the publication.

C. E. Lester revisited the topic of Sam Houston again in 1855, 1866 and 1883, expanding on what was written here in the first edition. We can surmise two things from its publication history. The first is that Houston as subject matter sold books, or else Lester wouldn't have kept producing more Houston bios. The second thing we learn about is Sam's likely view of the book. Lester published this, the 1846 edition, under his own name, but he didn't claim authorship to the next edition published while Houston was alive and seeking a presidential nomination, nor did he claim authorship to the one immediately following Houston's death. Those were published anonymously. Only the first edition (1846) and the final edition (published two decades after Houston's death) bear Lester's name. And only in the final edition did Lester publish his tale of working in Houston's hotel room and being intimate friends with him for twenty years. Lester was a man who relished seeing his name in the headlines, yet he avoided attaching his name to future Houston biographies until the subject had been in the ground for a very long time. This may give us the best clue we have as to how General Houston felt about this biographer. Did the Houston camp reach out to Lester privately? Did the author and the subject cross paths in Washington? Something pushed Lester to remove his name from future Sam bios.

One reviewer remarked that a better title would have been *The Life of A Drunkard by A Liar*. Of course, Houston was sober by this point but the rest of that title does hold some water. C. Edwards Lester was one shady hombre. Let's take a peek at Houston's first biographer.

Charles Edwards Lester was born in 1815 in Connecticut. He began public life as a Presbyterian minister and vocal abolitionist in

New York. In 1840, he was elected a delegate to the World Anti-Slavery Convention held in London. He hobnobbed there, even giving his surname as Leicester hoping to endear himself to the Brits. But the abolition game didn't pay the desired dividends, so he jumped ship. He dropped the "Reverend" from his name and began to move in political circles. In 1841, based on his brief visit to London, he wrote a book called *The Glory and Shame of England,* assailing England for being unkind to the U. S. and for having a state-established religion. Folks on both sides of the Atlantic were quick to point out that Lester had merely plagiarized other anti-England tracts and had fabricated most of his firsthand adventures across the pond.

In 1842, he was appointed U. S. consul to Genoa, Italy. While serving there, he attempted to broker a deal with descendants of Amerigo Vespucci. Lester, who told the Vespucci clan that he was a relative of President Polk and had familial sway, was entrusted with an antique painting of the famous Vespucci. Mr. Lester was to offer the United States the painting as a gift from the explorer's family, and attach a plea that America grant the poor Vespuccis some land on this continent as a thank you gesture. Lester instead told the family that Congress had rejected the painting and attempted to sell it in Boston.

Publication announcements for this book were released amidst the controversy that C. E. Lester had fabricated much of his last book—also a biography "authorized" by the subject. Lester claimed to have spent lots of quality time with famous American-born sculptor Hiram Powers in Italy, jotting down their conversations, then transcribing them into book form. He claimed he did all of this with Powers' knowledge, consent and assistance. Powers publicly objected to the book, saying that he didn't say half of what was published and certainly didn't have a role in editing the manuscript, as Lester had claimed. Scandal ensued and Lester was again labeled a charlatan.

Lester published several classic works of Italian prose translated to English, claiming the translations as his own. It was revealed in 1847 that he hadn't translated a single syllable himself. He had a young Polish polyglot in his employ, to whom he paid a pittance to do all the translating.

After he was discharged from his consular duties in 1847, it became known that Consul Lester had been pilfering from the piggy bank of the American Consulate at Genoa. Not long after his return to the U. S., the former abolitionist was advocating for the Compromise of 1850 and pushing for strict enforcement of the Fugitive Slave Act. He began a newspaper in New York City to that end and was excoriated by the abolitionist movement for it. He then slid into the Know Nothing party, of which Houston was also a member at the time. In 1854, he wrote a very Know Nothing (anti-Catholic) novel under the pseudonym Helen Dhu. One New York paper reviewed it by simply saying, "Helen don't."

As the anonymous American political correspondent to the London *Times* in the 1850s, Lester supported Franklin Pierce's presidential bid in glowing tones. In fact, he raved about Pierce until the newly elected executive completed his cabinet appointments. Then the raving turned to ranting, and it came to light that Lester, the former consul, was the anonymous correspondent. Feeling dejected after not receiving the cabinet post or consular appointment for which he had lobbied, Lester turned his pen against President Pierce, calling him and his cabinet "enemies of the United States." Language like that plays well on Twitter in 2019, but such inflammatory rhetoric was considered outrageous in the 1850s, with the Union on the brink of fracture.

Lester was working for the Census Bureau in 1860, and drinking heavily when the Civil War came on. He applied for a clerk job with the War Department and worked in that capacity until 1863, when he was arrested and detained on the suspicion that he was a Confederate spy. In reality, he was just a drunk. He claimed that he had a carbuncle on his leg that needed lancing—a contrived excuse to go on a bender. Because of his position, he had War Department papers on him when he was arrested for public drunkenness near the Virginia border. He was released after a stint in jail in Washington and fully acquitted.

Four years before his death, Charles Edwards Lester consigned his collection of autographs and fine art prints to a New York City auctioneer. The only item relating to Sam Houston is a letter about Houston family history and doesn't seem to bear Sam's signature, according to the 1886 catalog. No other Houston correspondence was auctioned, although the men supposedly shared two decades of friendship and the Lester family was in need of funds.

Mr. Lester died in Detroit on January 29, 1890 at the age of 74. Among the single-line death notices, I found a few actual obituaries. Among them, this one from the Chicago *Herald*, which reads, in part:

> Lester was a very remarkable man in his day...In 1862, he was in Washington, doing nothing, and the slave of an appetite for alcohol. At that time, he was about 45 years of age, tall, elegantly formed, with light hair, a complexion once evidently fresh, but then approaching the color of sole leather, and a face seamed with 1,000 wrinkles, as if dug with the point of a fine needle. His eyes were a mild gray, his features regular and mobile, and his bearing erect and dignified.

> Lester, drunk or sober, was one of the finest conversationalists in the world. No subject whatever was foreign to his ability to describe or discuss. He knew all men and places. He was as familiar with authors living and dead as the average man is with the alphabet. His style varied with the subject of his conversation. Now he was calm, equable, dignified; again his words rushed out, a torrent of fiery enthusiasm, or he spoke in a low tone, broken with sobs, while his face was bathed with tears.

> Where or how he lived in Washington nobody knew. He had no business and spent most of his time at Willard's Hotel awaiting an invitation to drink. He spoke of his family with pride and never of his wife save with profound respect...He was an author, a poet, a diplomat, a philosopher, a statesman, a gentleman, and—a bummer.

We all know Sam Houston's achievements and sins. The things we don't know about Houston, this book doesn't help us to know. Texas historians ought to consider this, the first biography of Sam Houston, less of a biography and something more akin to fan fiction. It's an archetypal hero's journey written by an archetypal nineteenth century mountebank.

-Michelle M. Haas
North Padre Island

A WORD TO THE READER
BEFORE HE BEGINS THE BOOK OR THROWS IT DOWN.

I have lived to see obloquy heaped by the Sons of the Puritans upon an outraged People bravely struggling for Independence, in the holy name of liberty.

I have lived to see unmeasured calumny poured on the head of an heroic Man who struck the fetter from his bleeding country on the field, and preserved her by his counsels in the Cabinet. And I have lived to do justice to that man and that People by asserting the truth.

This book will lose me some friends, but it will win me better ones in their places. But if it lost me all and gained me none, in God's name, as I am a free man, I would publish it.

I am no man's partizan, or eulogist but I dare tell the truth to the men of my own times, and leave the men of other times to take care of my reputation. I do not ask the Reader to adopt my opinions—but I do ask him to weigh my facts. I deprecate no Critic's severity; I only say to him as the old Greek did to the man with the uplifted club: "Strike, sir, but hear me first." Let us see if any good thing can come out of Nazareth!

C. EDWARDS LESTER.

New York, 25TH August, 1846.

CHAPTER I:
THE HERO-PEOPLE

There are moments in our lives, on which fortune loves to hang all our future history; and, when we meet the crisis like men, she takes care of the future for us. Once past the hour of trial, there are no more hardships to undergo, no more dangers to encounter. The gates, which guard the way to glory, are swung wide open to the advancing hero, and he treads the path of light and triumph, as the Roman conqueror marched up to the temple of Jupiter through the streets of the Eternal City.

So, too, there are days in the lives of nations, when fortune loves to suspend the glory of a people upon a single hour—when they are called on to decide what their future history shall be—whether their banners shall float over new empires, extending their liberty, laws, and civilization over oppressed and benighted millions, crushing old structures of despotism, breaking the arm of the tyrant, and melting away the rotten fabrics of hoary superstitions, to emancipate whole peoples—or, whether the wheels of their national greatness, like the sun of Joshua, shall stand still in mid heaven, and the solemn proclamation go forth, that they have reached the farthest limits of their civilization—that the race of their daring young men is suddenly arrested—that there shall be no new field for untrodden adventure and lofty achievement—that the world, and even despotism itself, may roll its wheels of conquest up to their frontier borders, and enlarge the empire of tyranny and superstition at its will, for they have done their work. They have extended the bright circle of their freedom and power till they can extend it no longer. No bold woodsman may pass their limits, and plunge off into the wilds, to cut out for himself and his children a home in *God's* own forests, for his government will never protect the squatter adventurer, albeit the James River settler, and the uncompromising Puritan, were nothing more.

And if so be one after another of these forest Heroes has led the way through the green woods beyond the Sabine, and they can at last show the traveler the smoke of ten thousand new cottages, wreathing up into the clear blue sky of New Estramadura; and if so be this new race of Puritans, Cavaliers, Huguenots, Catholics and Outlaws, all fraternally mingled, have built up the beautiful fabric of a new free commonwealth, for all the world to come to for a home, and done it withal while they were protecting their wives and little children from savages, made remorseless by Puritan *fire-water*, and from the enervated, but perfidious Mexicans—why, even after these Hunter-Legislators, these Squatter-Founders of States, have done all the hard work, this old republic, whose wheels can roll no further, will not even accept, what no other nation ever had to offer, the free gift of a mighty domain declared independent, as New York and Virginia were seventy years ago, although the offering be made without money and without price.

Yes, these trial days come to nations as they come to men. One of those Rubicon-hours came on the cold bleak Rock of Plymouth, where a little band of liberty-loving men landed, under the cover of a keen northern blast, to begin the great business for which Anglo-Saxons crossed the Atlantic, of founding free commonwealths. Virginia, too, had her hour, and her Cavaliers went through Indian-haunted woods, as Marshal Ney's cavalry charged through the Black Forest.

At last, after much debate and more stupid misconception, the New Republic, *par excellence*, came and laid on our federal altars her young shield. It was riddled with rifle-bullets, and battered by the trenchant strokes of the tomahawk. You need not have looked very close to have seen, too, the ghostly image of Mexican treachery filling up the interstices. What an offering was this! A young hero-people, a new Rome, coming out of the forests, walking in light, and clothed in strength, and advancing in manliness up to our altars.

When the future historian shall tell his readers that the Young Republic was driven away from our Capitol, and her shield hurled back in her face, they will not believe it. That the Representatives of America debated, hesitated, laughed Texas to scorn, will, to the next generation, seem a malignant invention of the historian. But it was so, and the last resource of republicanism was resorted to. The Texian banner was flung to the breeze, and the *People* of this country were asked to settle the question. And over the hills of New England, the rallying cry rang where the young American Eagle first unfurled his wings, and far up the Valley of the Mississippi, and down to the Florida coast, and back came the glorious shout of a grateful welcome, and Texas came into the Union.

It was a proud day when her Senators took their seats. Greatest, and most daring of all the Texians, came that wondrous man, who had stood by the side of the Young Republic, leaning on his rifle, and rocked her infancy in those far-off wilds. Yes, there he stood, on the threshold of the Senate Chamber, bringing in his arms, not like the triumphant Generals of Rome, the fine gold or precious stones of distant barbaric princes, lashed to his victorious car, but a new and a vast empire. There stood the tall, erect, ample form of the care-worn chieftain—his locks turned prematurely grey by the hardships of a revolutionary frontier life. His wounds were upon him, for he had bled freely in the service of two Republics. Let us inquire something of the history of this Man.

CHAPTER II:
The Beginning of Life

Gen. Sam Houston was born the 2d. of March, 1793, in Rockbridge County, Virginia, seven miles east of Lexington, at a place known as Timber Ridge Church. The day of his birth, he was, many years afterwards, to celebrate as the anniversary of the birth of a new Republic—for it was on his natal day that Texas declared herself, by the grace of God, and her own brave riflemen, free and independent.

His ancestors, on his father's and mother's side, are traced back to the Highlands of Scotland. They are there found fighting for "God and Liberty," by the side of John Knox. During those times of trouble, they emigrated with that numerous throng of brave men and women who were driven away from their Highland homes, to seek a refuge in the North of Ireland. Here they remained till the siege of Derry, in which they were engaged, when they emigrated to Pennsylvania. For more than a century, these families seemed to have kept together in all their wanderings, and at last a union was formed between them by the marriage of his parents, who had been some time settled in Virginia, when the birth of the subject of these pages took place.

His father was a man of moderate fortune; indeed, he seems to have possessed only the means of a comfortable subsistence. He was known only for one passion, and this was for a military life. He had borne his part in the Revolution, and was successively the Inspector of Gen. Bowyer's and Gen. Moore's Brigades. The latter post he held till his death, which took place in 1807, while he was on a tour of inspection among the Alleghany Mountains. He was a man of powerful frame, fine bearing, and indomitable courage. These qualities his son inherited, and they were the only legacy he had to leave him.

His mother was an extraordinary woman. She was distinguished by a full, rather tall, and matronly form, a fine carriage, and an impressive and dignified countenance. She was gifted with intellectual and moral qualities, which elevated her in a still more striking manner above most of her sex. Her life shone with purity and benevolence, and yet she was nerved with a stern fortitude which never gave way in the midst of the wild scenes that chequer the history of the frontier settler. Her beneficence was universal, and her name was called with gratitude by the poor and the suffering. Many years afterward, her son returned from his distant exile to weep by her bedside when she came to die.

Such were the parents of this Man. Those who know his history will not be astonished to find that they were of that noble race which first subdued the wildness of Virginia and Tennessee forests, and the ferocity of their savage inhabitants. It is a matter of some interest to inquire, what were the means of education offered to this Virginia boy. We have learned from all quarters, that he never could be got into a schoolhouse till he was eight years old, nor can we learn that he ever accomplished much in a literary way after he did enter. Virginia, which has never become very famous for her schools at any period, had still less to boast of forty years ago. The state made little or no provision by law for the education of its citizens, and each neighborhood was obliged to take care of its rising population. Long before this period, Washington College had been removed to Lexington, and a Field School was kept in the ruined old edifice once occupied by that institution. This school seems, from all accounts (and we have taken some pains to inform ourselves about this matter), to have been of doubtful utility. He is said, however, to have learned to read and write—to have gained some imperfect ideas of cyphering. Late in the fall and the winter, were the only seasons he was allowed to improve even the dubious advantages of such a school. The rest of the year he was kept to hard work. If he worked very well he was sometimes permitted to run home from the fields to be in time to retain his place in spelling. But it is doubtful if he ever went to such a school more than six months in all, till the death of his father, which took place when he was thirteen years old. This event changed at once the fortunes of the family. They had been maintained in comfortable circumstances, chiefly through the exertions of the father, and now they were to seek for other reliances.

Mrs. Houston was left with the heavy burden of a numerous family. She had six sons and three daughters. But she was not a woman to succumb to misfortune, and she immediately sold out the homestead and prepared to cross the Alleghany Mountains, and find a new home on the fertile banks of the Tennessee River. Those of our readers who live in the midst of a crowded population, surrounded by all that embellishes civilized life, may be struck with the heroism of a Virginia woman who, forty years ago, took up her journey through those unpeopled regions; and yet few of them can have any adequate conception of the hardships such a heroine had to encounter. We hope the day may come when our young authors will stop writing and dreaming about European castles, with their crazy knights and lady-loves, and hunting through the mummy-haunted halls of the pyramids, and set themselves to work to glean the unwritten legends of heroism and adventure, which the old men would tell them, who are now smoking their pipes around the roof-trees of Kentucky and Tennessee.

There is room for the imagination to play around the toilsome path of this widow and her children, as she pushed her adventurous way to her forest home. Some facts, too, of wild interest are in our possession—but we shall hurry on with our story, for, if we mistake not, our readers will find romance enough in this history to satisfy the wildest fancy.

Fired still with the same heroic spirit which first led them to try the woods, our daring little party stopped not till they reached the limits of the emigration of those days. They halted eight miles from the Tennessee river, which was then the boundary between white men and the Cherokee Indians.

Young Houston was now set to work with the rest of the family in breaking up the virgin soil, and providing the means of subsistence. There seems to have been very little fancy in his occupations now for some time; he became better acquainted than ever with what is called hard work,—a term which has a similar signification in all the languages and countries we happen to be acquainted with.

There was an academy established in that part of East Tennessee about this time, and he went to it for a while, just after Hon. Mr. Jarnagin, who now represents his State in the U. S. Senate, had left it. He had got possession, in some way, of two or three books, which had a great power over his imagination. No boy ever reads well till he feels a thirst for intelligence, and no surer indication is needed that this period has come, than to see the mind directed towards those gigantic heroes who rise like spectres from the ruins of Greece and Rome, towering high and clear above the darkness and gloom of the Middle Ages. He had, among other works, Pope's Iliad, which he read so constantly, we have been assured on the most reliable authority, he could repeat it almost entire from beginning to end. His imagination was now fully awakened, and his emulation began to be stirred. Reading translations from Latin and Greek soon kindled his desire to study those primal languages; and so decided did this propensity become, that on being refused when he asked the master's permission, he turned on his heel, and declared solemnly that he would never recite another lesson of any other kind while he lived—and from what we have been able to learn of his history, we think it very probable that he kept his word most sacredly! But he had gathered from the classic world more through Pope's Iliad than many a ghostly book-worm, who has read Euripides or Aeschylus among the solemn ruins of the Portico itself. He had caught "the wonted fire" that still "lives in the ashes" of their heroes, and his future life was to furnish the materials of an epic more wondrous than many a man's whose name has become immortal.

His elder brothers seem to have crossed his wishes occasionally, and by a sort of fraternal tyranny quite common, exercised over him some severe restraints. At last they compelled him to go into a merchant's store, and stand behind the counter. This kind of life he had little relish for, and he suddenly disappeared. A great search was made for him, but he was nowhere to be found for several weeks. At last intelligence reached the family that Sam had crossed the Tennessee river, and gone to live among the Indians, where, from all accounts, he seemed to be living much more to his liking. They found him, and began to question him on the motives for this novel proceeding. Sam was now, although so very young, nearly six feet high, and standing straight as an Indian, coolly replied that "he preferred measuring deer tracks to tape—that he liked the wild liberty of the red men better than the tyranny of his own brothers, and if he could not study Latin in the academy, he could, at least, read a translation from the Greek in the woods, and read it in peace. So they could go home as soon as they liked."

His family, however, thinking this a freak from which he would soon recover when he got tired of the Indians, gave themselves no great uneasiness about him. But week after week passed away, and Sam did not make his appearance. At last his clothes were worn out, and he returned to be refitted. He was kindly received by his mother, and for awhile his brothers treated him with due propriety. But the first act of tyranny they showed drove him to the woods again, where he passed entire months with his Indian mates, chasing the deer through the forest with a fleetness little short of their own, engaging in all those gay sports of the happy Indian boys, and wandering along the banks of the streams by the side of some Indian maiden, sheltered by the deep woods, conversing in that universal language which finds its way to the heart. From a strange source we have learned much of his Indian history during these three or four years, and in the absence of facts it would be no difficult matter to fancy what must have been his occupations. It was the moulding period of life, when the heart, just charmed into the fevered hopes and dreams of youth, looks wistfully around on all things for light and beauty—"when every idea of gratification fires the blood and flashes on the fancy—when the heart is vacant to every fresh form of delight, and has no rival engagements to withdraw it from the importunities of a new desire." The poets of Europe, in fancying such scenes, have borrowed their sweetest images from the wild idolatry of the Indian maiden. Houston has since seen nearly all there is in life to live for, and yet he has been heard to say that, as he looks back over the waste of life, there's nothing half so sweet to remember as this sojourn he made among the untutored children of the forest.

And yet this running wild among the Indians, sleeping on the ground, chasing wild game, making love to Indian maidens, and reading Homer's Iliad withal, seemed a pretty strange business, and people used to say that Sam Houston would either be a great Indian chief, or die in a mad-house, or be Governor of the State—for it was very certain that *some* dreadful thing would overtake him!

Well, it may have been doubtful, and it was for a long time, what all this would end in. But the mystery has cleared away, somewhat, since the battle of San Jacinto. Certain it is that his early life among the Indians was, as the event proved, a necessary portion of that wonderful training that fitted him for his strange destiny. There it was he became initiated into the profound mysteries of the red man's character, and a taste was formed for wild forest life, which, made him, many years after, abandon once more the habitations of civilized men, with their coldness, their treachery, and their vices, and pass years among the children of the Great Spirit, till he finally led the way to the achievement of the independence of a great domain and the consolidation of a powerful commonwealth.

Guided by a wisdom all His own, the Ruler of Nations led him by an unknown path, and his wild history reminds us of the story of Romulus, who was nurtured by the beasts of the forest till he planted the foundation of a mighty empire. With the history of the Father of Rome, the pen of poets has played—and it would seem, after all, to have been but a prophecy in fable, whose fulfillment the world has waited for till our days. Certain it is, too, that no man has ever lived on this continent (whose history we know) who has had so complete a knowledge of the Indian character—none who could sway so powerful a control over the savage mind. During his entire administration of the government of Texas, not an Indian tribe violated a treaty with the Republic; and it is nearly as safe to say, that during the administration of others, not a tribe was known to make or regard one.

During the latter part of June (just past), General Morehead arrived at Washington with forty wild Indians from Texas—belonging to more than a dozen tribes. We saw their meeting with Gen. Houston. One and all ran to him and clasped him in their brawny arms, and hugged him like bears to their naked breasts, and called him Father—beneath the copper skin and thick paint, the blood rushed, and their faces changed, and the lip of many a warrior trembled, although the Indian may not weep. These wild men knew him and revered him as one who was too directly descended from the Great Spirit, to be approached with familiarity, and yet they loved him so well they could not help it. These were the men "he had been," in the fine language of Acquiquosk, whose words we quote, "too subtle for, on the war path—too powerful in battle, too magnanimous in victory, too wise in council, and too true in faith." They had flung away their arms in Texas, and with the Comanche Chief who headed their file, they had come to Washington to see their Father. I said these iron warriors shed no tears, when they met their old friend—but white men who stood by will tell us what they did. We were there, and we have

witnessed few scenes in which mingled more of what is called
the moral sublime. In the gigantic form of Houston, on whose
ample brow the beneficent love of a father was struggling with
the sternness of the patriarch warrior, we saw civilization aw-
ing the savage at its feet. We needed no interpreter to tell us
that this impressive supremacy was gained in the forest.

But we have quite lost the thread of our story. This wild
life among the Indians lasted till his eighteenth year. He had,
during his visits once or twice a year to his family, to be refitted
in his dress, purchased many little articles of taste or utility to
use among the Indians. In this manner, he had incurred a debt
which he was bound in honor to pay. To meet this engagement, he had no other resource left but to abandon his "dusky
companions," and teach the children of pale-faces. As may
naturally be supposed, it was no easy matter for him to get a
school, and on the first start, the enterprise moved very slowly.
But as the idea of abandoning anything on which he had once
fixed his purpose, was no part of his character, he persevered,
and in a short time he had more scholars to turn away, than
he had at first to begin with. He was also paid what was considered an exorbitant price. Formerly, no master had hinted
above $6 per annum. Houston, who probably thought that one
who had been graduated at an Indian university ought to hold
his lore at a dearer rate, raised the price to $8—one-third to be
paid in corn, delivered at the mill, at 33½ cents per bushel—
one-third in cash, and one-third in domestic cotton cloth, of
variegated colors, in which our Indian Professor was dressed.
He also wore his hair behind, in a snug queue, and is said to
have been very much in love with it, probably from an idea
that it added somewhat to the adornment of his person—in
which, too, he probably was sadly mistaken.

When he had made money enough to pay his debts, he shut
up his school, and went back to his old master, to study. He
put Euclid into his hands. He carried that ugly, unromantic
book back and forth to and from the school a few days, without

trying to solve even so much as the first problem, and then he came to the very sensible conclusion, that he would never try to be a scholar! This was in 1813. But fortunately an event now took place which was to decide his fate.

The bugle had sounded, and for the second time, America was summoned to measure her strength with the Mistress of the Seas. A recruiting party of the United States Army came to Maryville, with music, a banner, and some well-dressed sergeants. Of course, young Houston enlisted—anybody could have guessed as much. His friends said he was ruined—that he must by no means join the army as a common soldier. He then made his first speech, as far as we can learn:— "And what have your craven souls to say about *the ranks?*—Go to hell with your stuff; I would much sooner honor the ranks, than disgrace an appointment. You don't know me now, but you shall hear of me."

His old friends and acquaintances, considering him hopelessly disgraced, cut his acquaintance at once. His mother gave her consent, standing tall and matronly in the door of her cottage, as she handed her boy the musket: "There, my son, take this musket," she said, "and never disgrace it: for remember, I had rather all my sons should fill one honorable grave, than that one of them should turn his back to save his life. Go, and remember, too, that while the door of my cottage is open to brave men, it is eternally shut against cowards."

He marched off. He was soon promoted to a sergeant. In a short time he became the best drill in the regiment;—soon after, he was marched to Fort Hampton, at the head of the Muscle Shoals, in Alabama, where he was promoted to an ensign. Returned to Knoxville—assisted in drilling and organizing the Eastern Battalion of the 39th Regiment of Infantry; and from thence marched to the Ten Islands, where he remained encamped for some time. The line of march was then taken up for Fort Williams. The Regiment descended the Coosa, and marched for To-Ho-Pe-Ka, or the Horse-Shoe, where some events took place, deserving a more minute relation.

CHAPTER III:
The Soldier

Most of our readers are doubtless familiar with the history of the great battle of the Horse-Shoe. An indecisive struggle had for a long time been carried on with the Creek Indians, who had avoided the hazards of open warfare, hoping at last, by forest ambuscades and stealthy eruptions, to weary out a foe they did not dare to meet in a general engagement. But this kind of warfare was soon to be brought to an end. They had a foe to contend with, who out-matched them in subtlety, and all the daring impetuosity of his nature was bent upon their destruction.

General Jackson's army encamped at Fort Williams, now amounted to more than two thousand men, and his spies were scattered far and wide through the forests. Retreating from village to village and point to point, the enemy had gathered all their effective force on a bend of the Tallapoosa, where a thousand warriors—the chivalry of the Creek Nation—following the guidings of their prophets, had taken their last stand, resolved to risk all upon a single struggle. This bend, which they called To-ho-pe-ka, or the Horse-Shoe, is accurately described by its name. It is a peninsula of about one hundred acres of land, opening on the north, where it was protected by a massive breast-work, reaching down to the river on both sides, composed of three tiers of heavy pine logs, with two rows of skilfully arranged port-holes.

On the morning of the 27th of March Gen. Jackson reached the Horse-Shoe, and immediately prepared for action. In a few hours, by a masterly arrangement of his forces, he had completely invested the peninsula. Gen. Coffee had, early in

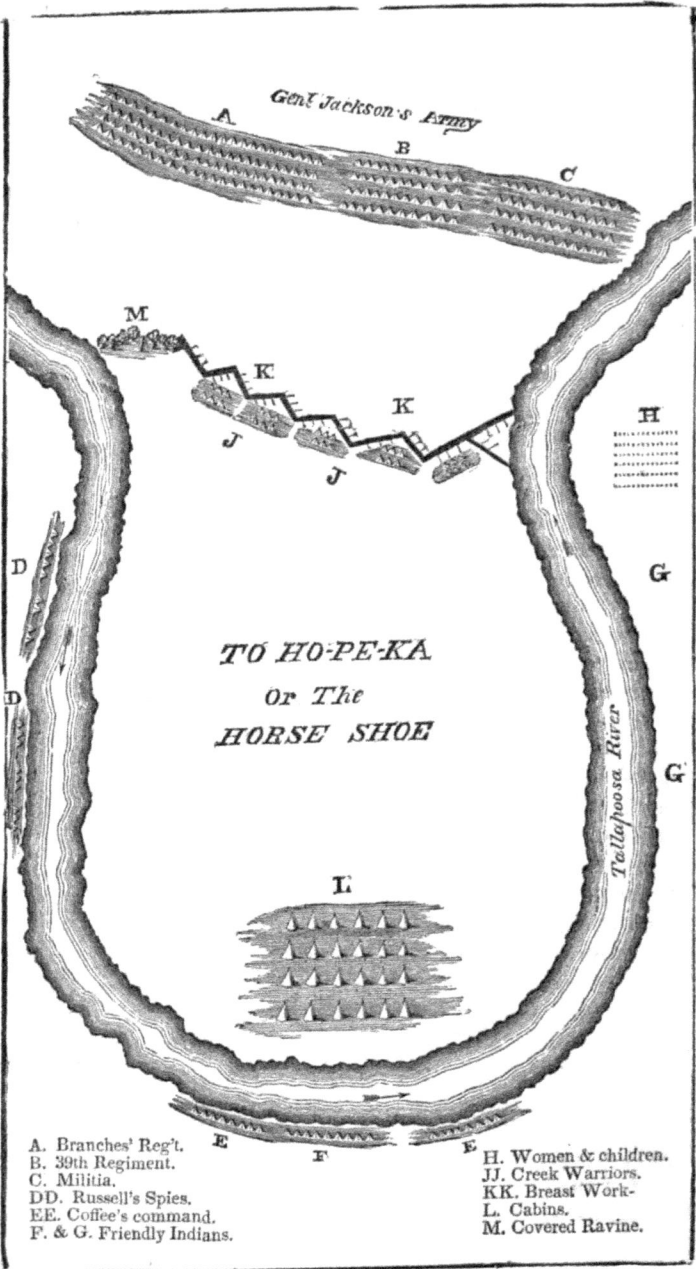

Gen.ˡ Jackson's Army

A
B
C

M
K
K
J
J
H

D

D

G

TÓ HO-PE-KA
Or The
HORSE SHOE

Tallapoosa River

G

L

E
F
E

A. Branches' Reg't.
B. 39th Regiment.
C. Militia.
DD. Russell's Spies.
EE. Coffee's command.
F. & G. Friendly Indians.
H. Women & children.
JJ. Creek Warriors.
KK. Breast Work.
L. Cabins.
M. Covered Ravine.

the morning, crossed the river at a ford two miles below, with a body of mounted men and nearly all the force of friendly Indians, serving under Gen. Jackson, and at ten o'clock he had drawn up his lines on the south of the bend, cutting off all escape from three sides of the peninsula. In the meantime, the General had advanced towards the north side of the bend, with the main army, and drawing up his lines, he ordered the two pieces of artillery to play upon the Indian breastworks. The first gun was fired at about half-past ten o'clock, and a brisk fire maintained till nearly one, apparently without much effect, the small cannon shot playing almost harmlessly against massive timbers. No opportunity had yet been given to the main army to show their valor; but a rattle of musketry mingling with the sharp crack of a hundred rifles was heard, and a heavy column of smoke came rolling up from the southern part of the peninsula.

The Cherokees, under Gen. Coffee, had discovered a line of canoes half concealed by the bushes on the opposite shore, and in a few minutes they swam the stream and brought them across. Richard Brown, their gallant chief, leaped into a canoe, followed by his brave Cherokees, and with Capt. Russell's companies of spies crossed the river. They first set fire to the cluster of wigwams near the shore, and, as the smoke rose over them, advanced upon the rear of a thousand warriors who were sheltered from the artillery on the north.

When Gen. Jackson's troops heard the firing and saw the smoke, they knew that their companions had crossed the river, and they were impatient to storm the breastworks. But the General held them steady in their lines till he had sent an interpreter to remove all the women and children in the peninsula, amounting to several hundreds, to a safe place beyond the river. The moment this was effected, he gave an order to storm the breastworks. The order was received with a shout, and the 39th Regiment under Col. Williams, and Gen. Doherty's brigade of East Tennesseans, rushed up with loud cries to the breastwork, where a short but bloody struggle followed at the port-holes, bayonet to bayonet and muzzle to muzzle. Major Montgomery was the first man to spring upon the breast-works, but a ball in the head hurled him back. About the same instant, on the extreme right of the 39th Regiment, Ensign Houston scaled the breastworks, calling out to his brave follows to follow him as he leaped down among the Indians cutting his way.

While he was scaling the works, or soon after he reached the ground, a barbed arrow struck deep into his thigh. He kept his ground for a moment till his lieutenant and men were by his side, and the warriors had begun to recoil under their desperate onset. He then called to his lieutenant to extract the arrow, after he had tried in vain to do it himself. The officer made two unsuccessful attempts and failed—"Try again," said Houston, the sword with which he was still keeping the command raised over his head, "and if you fail this time I will smite you to the earth." With a desperate effort he drew forth the arrow, tearing the flesh as it came. A stream of blood rushed from the place, and Houston crossed the breastworks to have his wounds dressed. The surgeon bound it up and staunched the blood, and Gen. Jackson, who came up to see who had been wounded, recognizing his young ensign, ordered him firmly not to return. Under any other circumstances Houston would have obeyed any order from the brave man who stood over him, but now he begged the general to allow him to return to his men. Gen. Jackson ordered him most peremptorily not to cross the breastworks again. But Houston was determined to die in that battle or win the fame of a hero. He remembered how the finger of scorn had been pointed at him as he fell into the ranks of the recruiting party that marched through the village, and rushing once more to the breastworks, he was in a few seconds at the head of his men.

The action had now become general, and more than two thousand men were struggling hand to hand. Arrows and spears and balls were flying, swords and tomahawks were gleaming in the sun, and the whole peninsula rang with the yell of the savage, and the groans of the dying.

The thousand warriors who had gathered there that day were chosen men. A brother of Tecumseh had some months before visited all the villages of the Creek nation and stirred up their passions for blood and revenge, proclaiming to their prophets that the voice of the Great Spirit had called him to go on the mission, and that the flower of their people must assemble to give battle to the pale faces, and the day should be crowned with the final destruction of their foes. There was in this strange mission enough of mystery to inflame all the superstition and malignity of the nation, and following their prophets, they had at last met the pale faces on the day that would give victory to their people. The day of the battle had come, and warriors by hundreds were falling; but they were firm in the belief of their prophets, who still proclaimed that they should win the day. The Great Spirit, they said, would sweep their enemies away with a storm of wrath, and his signal should be a cloud from heaven. And it is proper to add, that when the struggle was decided, and the commander-in-chief was issuing an order to stop the carnage, and had sent an interpreter to tell the foe their lives should be spared if they would surrender, a cloud suddenly overspread the sky. The superstitious warriors, believing it the signal of their promised redemption, fired upon the interpreter after his message was delivered, and again the action began.

But the eagerly-watched signal ended in a quiet April shower, and no deliverance came to the brave, but devoted people. Not a warrior offered to surrender, even while the sword was at his breast. Hundreds had already fallen, and were weltering in their gore—multitudes of others had been shot or drowned, in attempting to swim the river—the ground of the peninsula was covered only with the dead and dying, and the battle was supposed to be over. To the last moment, the old prophets stood firm, and gazed up towards the sky; around them warriors clustered, feeling to the very last moment that relief would come. Hope expired only with the expiring groan of the last prophet, and the warrior who gasped at his side.

But the victory was still incomplete—the work of slaughter was not yet done. A large party of Indians had secreted themselves in a part of the breastworks, constructed over a ravine in the form of the roof of a house, with narrow port-holes, from which a murderous fire could be kept up, whenever the assailants should show themselves. Here the last remnant of the Creek warriors of the peninsula was gathered, and as the artillery could not be brought to bear upon the place, they could be dislodged only by a bold charge, which would probably cost the life of the brave men who made it.

An offer of life, if they would surrender, had been rejected with scorn by these brave, desperate savages, which sealed their fate. General Jackson now called for a body of men to make the charge. As there was no order given, the lines stood still, and not an officer volunteered to lead the forlorn hope. Supposing some captain would lead forward his company, Houston would wait no longer. Calling on his platoon to follow him, he dashed down the precipitous descent towards the covered ravine. But his men hesitated. With a desperation which belongs only to such occasions, he seized a musket from one of his men, and, leading the way, ordered the rest to follow him. There was but one way of attack that could prevail—it was to charge through the port-holes, although they were bristling with rifles and arrows, and it had to be done by a rapid, simultaneous plunge. As he was stopping to rally his men, and had leveled his musket, within five yards of the port-holes, he received two rifle-balls in his right shoulder, and his arm fell shattered to his side. Totally disabled, he turned and called once more to his men, and implored them to make the charge. But they did not advance. Houston stood in his blood till he saw it would do no good to stand any longer, and then went beyond the range of the bullets, and sank down exhausted to the earth. The Indians were at last dislodged from the covered ravine by its being set on fire. The sun was going down, and it set over the ruin of the Creek nation. Where, but a few hours before, a thousand brave savages had scowled on death and their assailants, there was nothing to be seen but volumes of dense smoke, rising heavily over the corpses of painted warriors, and the burning ruins of their fortifications.

After all the perils of this hard-fought engagement, in which he had displayed a heroism that excited the admiration of the entire army, and received wounds which are to this day unhealed, he was taken from the field of the dead and wounded, and committed to the hands of the surgeon. One ball was extracted, but no attempt was made to extract the other, for the surgeon said it was unnecessary to torture him, since he could not survive till the next morning. He spent the night as soldiers do, who war in the wilderness, and carry provisions in their knapsacks for a week's march. Comforts were out of the question for all; but Houston received less attention than the others, for everybody looked on him as a dying man, and what could be done for any, they felt should be done for those who were likely to live. It was the darkest night of his life, and it closed in upon the most brilliant day he had yet seen. We can fancy to ourselves what must have been the feelings of the young soldier, as he lay on the damp earth, through the hours of that dreary night, racked with the keen torture of his many wounds, and deserted in what he supposed was his dying hour.

But God, whose mysterious Providence guides its chosen instruments by a way they know not, had yet other work for him to do—he was yet to pass through many scenes of excitement and heroism; and, at last, to lead a brave band of pioneers triumphantly through all their struggles and sufferings to the peaceful enjoyment of a free commonwealth. The military prowess and heroism Houston displayed throughout that bloody day, secured for him the lasting regard of General Jackson, whose sympathies followed him through all his fortunes. More than thirty years after, when the venerable old Chief was trembling on the verge of life, looking out with un-dimmed cheerfulness from the dark inn of mortality upon the summer path of light that opened before him, he sent for General Houston to hurry to his bed-side to see him die.

On the following day, Houston was started on a litter, with the other wounded, for Fort Williams, some 60 or 70 miles distant. Here he remained, suspended between life and death, for a long time, neglected and exposed, the other regular officers of the regiment having all been removed to Fort Jackson or the Hickory Ground. He was taken care of, a part of the time, by Gen. Johnson, father of the present Postmaster General, and by Col. Cheatham, and by them at last brought back to the Ten Islands, and from thence by Gen. Dougherty, who commanded the Brigade from East Tennessee, through the Chero-kee Nation, to his mother's house in Blount County, where he arrived in the latter part of May, nearly two months after the battle of the Horse-Shoe.

This long journey was made in a litter, borne by horses, while he was not only helpless, but suffering the extremest agony. His diet was of the coarsest description, and most of the time he was not only deprived of medical aid, but even of those simple remedies which would at least have alleviated his sufferings. His toilsome way was through the forests, where he was obliged to encamp out, and often without shelter. No one around him had any expectation he would ever recover. At last, when he reached the house of his mother, he was so worn to a skeleton, that she declared she never would have known him to be her son, but for his eyes, which still retained something of their wonted expression.

Under the hospitable roof of that cottage, whose "door was always open to brave men," he languished a short time, and when he had recovered a little strength, went to Maryville for convenience to medical aid. Here his health gradually declined, and in quest of a more skillful surgeon, he was removed to Knoxville, 16 miles to the eastward. The physician to whom he applied found him in so low a state that he was unwilling to take charge of him, for he declared that he could only live a few days. But at the end of this period, finding he had not only survived, but begun to improve a little, the doctor offered his services, and he seemed to be slowly recovering.

When he had become strong enough to ride a horse, he set out by short journeys for Washington. He reached the seat of government soon after the burning of the Capitol. In common with every true friend of his country, his blood boiled when he saw the ruin that *heroic* people had worked, and he experienced one of the keenest pangs of his life, in the thought that his right arm should be disabled at such a moment, and while the foe was still prowling through the country. Winter was now advancing, and with his wounds still festering, he journeyed on to Lexington, Virginia, where he remained till early spring.

Having, as he supposed, sufficiently recovered to be able to do duty as a soldier in some situation, he prepared to cross the mountains. When he reached Knoxville, on his way to report himself ready for duty, he heard the glorious news of the Battle of New Orleans. His furlough had been unlimited.

After peace was proclaimed, he was stationed at the cantonment of his regiment, near Knoxville, and when the army was reduced, he was retained in the service as a Lieutenant, and attached to the 1st Regt. of Infantry, and stationed at New Orleans.

In the fall, he had embarked on the Cumberland, in a small skiff, in company with two young men, one of whom afterwards became distinguished as Gov. White, of Louisiana. He was then a beardless boy, just leaving college. They passed down the Cumberland, entered the Ohio, and at last found their way to the Mississippi, over whose mighty waters they floated through that vast solitude, which was then unbroken by the noise of civilized life. Our voyager had with him a few of those volumes which have been the companions of so many great and good men: a Bible, given to him by his mother, Pope's translation of the Iliad, the same book he had kept by him during his wild life among the Indians—Shakespeare, Akenside, and a few of those standard works of fiction, which, like Robinson Crusoe, Pilgrim's Progress, and the Vicar of Wakefield, have become a part of the history of every man who knows how to read. It is not difficult to imagine the effect such works must have produced upon the heated imagination of a young American soldier, voyaging through those impressive solitudes.

After many days their skiff turned a bend in the Mississippi, above Natchez, and far down the river they saw a vessel coming up the stream without sails, sending up a heavy column of smoke. Instead of being a vessel on fire, as they at first supposed, it turned out to be the first steamboat that ever went up the Mississippi river.

At Natchez they exchanged their skiff for the steamboat, and in eight days they reached New Orleans, where Houston reported for duty.

He now had his wounds operated on once more, and the operation nearly cost him his life. The rifle balls, after shattering most completely his right arm just below its juncture with the shoulder, had passed round and lodged near the shoulder blade. Nothing but an iron constitution had enabled him to endure the enormous suffering he had gone through, and the operation just performed had well nigh robbed him of his last strength. His lungs were supposed, moreover, to be irreparably injured; but that indomitable resolution which has borne him triumphantly through all the struggles of his stormy life, never gave way.

After a winter of extreme suffering, he sailed in April for New York, where he passed several weeks, with a slight improvement in health. Returning to Tennessee by the way of Washington, after visiting his friends, he reported to the Adjutant-General of the Southern Division, at Nashville, and was detailed on duty in the Adjutant's office, and stationed at Nashville from the 1st of January, 1817. He was attached to the office till the following November, when he was detailed on extra duty as a Sub-Indian agent among the Cherokee, to carry out the treaty just ratified with that nation. His feeble health rendered it peculiarly hazardous to encounter the exposures of such an agency, but Gen. Jackson considered it necessary to the public service that he should at least make the attempt, for he could procure the services of no one in whom he could repose such entire confidence. Accordingly, Lieut. Houston, yielding to the importunities of his commander, who, knowing he was unfit for public service, offered him a furlough if he should decline the agency, entered upon his new duties with ardor, and discharged them with marked ability. During that same winter he conducted a delegation of Indians to Washington. When he arrived at the seat of government, he found that attempts had been made to injure him with the government, for having prevented African negroes from being smuggled into the Western States from Florida, which was then a province of Spain. These reports had been circulated by the friends of the smugglers, who were then in Congress.

He vindicated himself before the President and the Secretary of War, and showed that in all he had done, he had only endeavored to secure respect for the laws of the country. He was still to show, too, most conclusively, that while he had been occupied laboriously in his new and difficult mission, which he had, as was confessed on all hands, discharged with singular ability, he had been suffering without respite from his painful wounds received in the service of his country. It was the opinion of General Jackson, and all who understood Houston's position and services at the time, that he was not only entitled to a full and ample exculpation from all blame (which was indeed accorded to him), but had a right to expect that his magnanimous sacrifices for the State should have met with a warmer recognition. But he considered himself slighted at the time; and he resigned his First Lieutenancy in the army,—at a period, too, when his health rendered it exceedingly doubtful how he was to gain a livelihood. But he acted on the principle he has so often illustrated, that no man should be an almoner upon the bounty of a State who cannot bring to its service talents and acquisitions which would procure higher emoluments in private life. He returned with the Delegation to the agency on Hi-Wassee, and then resigned his commission as Sub-Agent, and went to Nashville to read law.

CHAPTER IV:
THE CIVILIAN

Houston was now in his twenty-fifth year. He had played an heroic part in the national struggle just past,—he had become familiar with the hardships the frontier soldier has to encounter, he had seen the treachery and the coldness of artificial life, and he had passed years among the simple-hearted but stern children of the Great Spirit.

With a mind enriched by experience and observation, and a lofty aspiration for enduring fame, he abandoned the life of the soldier to pursue the calmer path of the civilian. In his wanderings in search of health, his pay in the army had been inadequate to his necessities, and he found himself burdened down by a load of debt. Before he began the study of the law, he sold the last piece of property he possessed, and appropriated the last farthing of the avails to the discharge of his debts; but a residuum of several hundred still remained unpaid—the balance, however, was soon discharged.

He entered the office of Hon. James Trimble, who told him that eighteen months of hard study would be necessary before he could be admitted to the bar. He began his studies in June, 1818. He read a few of the standard works prescribed in a course of law studies, and read them thoroughly. He grasped the great principles of the science, and they were fixed in his mind forever. There is a class of men who are made up like composite architecture of the details of beauty stolen from primitive orders; such men constitute the secondary formations of society, but the intellectual world, like the frame of nature, reposes upon nobler and more massive strata.

Those men who borrow their lights from others, never lead the human race through great crises—those who depend on the strength they gather from books or men, are never equal to lofty achievements. The minds which electrify the world generate their own fire; such men seldom shine in details—they have no time to attend to them, and they never feel the loss of these secondary lights. The bold mariner who ventures at once upon the open sea, and regulates his course by a few towering headlands and solitary lights that gleam from afar, can give little information to the coaster about the tiny bays that indent the shore, or the color of the pebbles that glitter on the beach. But he has marked on his chart the dangerous reefs and the great currents of the ocean, and he is at home with his noble vessel wherever the sun and the moon and the stars shine.

So it is with those who explore the fields of science. Some men cultivate such studies only to amass details, to use on appropriate occasions, while others enter them only to gather general principles which have a universal application; and in approaching these two classes, we discover as grand a difference as we do between one of those islands of the Pacific seas newly formed by the countless animalculae of the ocean, and the bold brow of the everlasting mountain.

We have used these illustrations only to convey more perfectly an idea of Houston's character. His teacher had prescribed eighteen months study. In one *third of the time* he was recommended to apply for license, and he was admitted with eclat. A few months' study had enabled him to pass a searching examination with great honor to himself and his new profession. He immediately purchased a small library on credit, and established himself in Lebanon, thirty miles east of Nashville, and began the practice of law. Soon after, he was appointed Adjutant-General of the State, with the rank of Colonel. In the meantime he followed up his studies, and the practice of his profession with earnestness, and so rapidly did he rise at the bar, that he was, in October of the same year, elected District Attorney of the Davidson District, which made it desirable he should take up his residence at Nashville.

He was obliged to come in collision with all the talent of one of the ablest bars of Western America. Every step he trod was new to him, but he was almost universally successful in prosecutions, and his seniors who rallied him upon his *recent* advancement and his *rawness* in the practice, never repeated their jokes.

They discovered to their mortification that neither many books nor much dull plodding could enable them to measure weapons with a man so gifted in rare good sense and penetrating genius. We have taken considerable pains to render ourselves familiar with the various steps of Houston's advancement till he reached the highest honors of the State. But we shall be obliged to pass rapidly over this portion of his history, in order to leave space to speak more minutely of his subsequent achievements. The labors of the District Attorney were unceasing, but the fees were so inconsiderable he resigned his post at the end of twelve months, and resumed the regular practice of his profession, in which he rose to great and sudden distinction.

In 1821 he was elected Major-General by the field officers of the division, which comprised two thirds of the State. In 1823 he was recommended to offer his name as a candidate for Congress. In the various official stations he had filled, he had won so much respect, and at the bar he had displayed such rare ability that he was elected to Congress without opposition. His course in the national legislature was warmly approved by his constituents, and he was returned the second time by an almost unanimous vote.

His course in Congress won for him the universal respect and confidence of the people of Tennessee, and in 1827 he was elected Governor of that State by a majority of over 12,000. His personal popularity was unlimited, and his accession to office found him without an opponent in the legislature.

In January, 1829, he married a young lady of respectable family and of gentle character. Owing to circumstances, about which far more has been conjectured than known by the world, the union seems to have been as unhappy as it was short. In less than three months a separation took place, which filled society with the deepest excitement. Various reports flew through the state, all of them unfounded, and some of them begotten by the sheerest malignity, which divided the people of the State into two hostile parties, and inflamed popular feeling to the last point of excitement. As usual on such occasions, those who were most busy in the affair were the very ones who knew least about the merits of the case, and had the least right to interfere.

But unfortunately for the peace of society, there is everywhere a class of impertinent busy-bodies, who make it their special business to superintend and pry into the domestic affairs of their neighbors; and as curiosity must be gratified at any expense to private character, and such persons always like to believe the worst, the secrets of no family are exempt from their malignant intrusions. These are the disturbers of the peace of society whom the law seldom punishes, although they perpetrate more crimes than highwaymen and assassins—burglars of the domestic tranquility of families—robbers of others' good name—assassins of the characters of the innocent.

Thinking, most probably, that they were doing her a kindness, the friends of the lady loaded the name of Houston with odium. He was charged with every species of crime man ever committed. The very ignorance of the community about the affair, by increasing the mystery which hung over it, only made it seem the more terrible. In the meantime, Houston did not offer a single denial of a single calumny—would neither vindicate himself before the public, nor allow his friends to do it for him. He sat quietly, and let the storm of popular fury rage on. From that day he has even among his confidential friends maintained unbroken silence, and whenever he speaks of the lady, he speaks of her with great kindness. Not a word has ever fallen from his lips that cast a shade upon her character; nor did he ever allow an unkind breath against her in his presence. Whatever may have been the truth of the matter, or whatever his friends may have known or conjectured, he had but one reply for them—"This is a painful but it is a private affair. I do not recognize the right of the public to interfere in it, and I shall treat the public just as though it had never happened. And remember that, whatever may be said by the lady or her friends, it is no part of the conduct of a gallant or a generous man to take up arms against a woman. If my character cannot stand the shock, let me lose it. The storm will soon sweep by, and time will be my vindicator."

He had been elected to every office he had held in the State by acclamation, and he determined instantly to resign his office as governor, and forego all his brilliant prospects of distinction, and exile himself from the habitations of civilized men—a resolution more likely to have been begotten by philosophy than by crime.

We have no apology to offer for this singular event. If we knew the truth we should tell it. If Houston acted culpably, it could not be expected he would become his own accuser. If he were the injured party, and chose to bear in silence his wrong and the odium that fell on him, he certainly betrayed no meanness of spirit, for he never asked the sympathy of the world. But notwithstanding his unbroken silence about the affair and the sacrifice of all his hopes, he was denounced by the journals of the day, and hunted down with untiring malignity by those who had the meanness to pursue a generous man in misfortune. After his determination to leave the country was known, they threatened him with personal violence. But in this he bearded and defied them.

But his friends did not desert him while the sun of his fortune was passing this deep eclipse. They gathered around him, and the streets of Nashville would have flowed with blood if Houston's enemies had touched a hair of his head. But such ruffians never execute their vows, when they have brave men to deal with, and Houston resigned his office, and taking leave of his friends, he quietly left the city of Nashville. He now turned his back upon the haunts of white men, and there was no refuge left for him but the forests. There he had a home, of which the reader has yet heard nothing; it was far away from civilized life.

While he was roving in his youth among the Cherokees, he had found a friend in their chief, who adopted him as his son, and gave him a corner in his wigwam. In the meantime, the chief with his tribe had removed from the Hi-Wassee country to Arkansas, and become king of the Cherokees, resident there. During their long separation, which had now lasted more than eleven years, they had never ceased to interchange tokens of their kind recollections. When, therefore, he embarked on the Cumberland, he thought of his adopted father, and he turned his face to his wigwam-home, knowing that he would be greeted there with the old chief's blessing.

CHAPTER V:

THE EXILE

His separation from his friends at the steamboat was a touching scene. He was a young man, for he had not passed his thirty-fifth year. He was in the vigor and strength of early manhood. He had filled the highest stations, and been crowned with the highest honors, his state could give. They knew the history of his early life, and they felt pride in his character. He was literally a man of the people, and they looked forward to his future advancement with all the pride of kindred feelings. A storm had suddenly burst upon his path, but they knew it would soon sweep by, bearing him to a higher and fairer eminence than before. He seemed to be casting from him the palm of victory; to be stepping down from his glory to obscurity, and his friends (and they were *the people of Tennessee*) parted from him with sorrow and in sadness.

And it was a strange sight to see one so young, around whose brow the myrtle wreath of fame was twining, cast aside the robes of office and give up a bright future for a home in the wilderness. It was no flight of a criminal; it was not even a necessary retirement from turbulence and excitement, for even before he left, the fury of his enemies had abated and his real strength was greater than ever. But it was a voluntary exile from scenes which only harrowed his feelings while he stayed, and the Almighty Providence, which had shaped out his future life, was leading him in a mysterious way through the forests to found a new empire. Let those who laugh at a Divine Providence, which watches over its chosen instruments, sneer as they read this; they may sneer on—they are welcome to their creed.

Landing at the mouth of the White River, he ascended the Arkansas to Little Rock, and then on alternately by land and water to the Falls of the Arkansas, four hundred miles to the northwest. The old chief's wigwam was built near the mouth of the Illinois, on the east side of the Arkansas, and the Cherokees were settled on both sides of the river above Fort Smith.

It was night when the steamboat, which carried Houston, arrived at the Falls, two miles distant from the dwelling of the Cherokee chief. As the boat passed the mouth of the river, intelligence was communicated to the old man that his adopted son Colenneh (the Raven—the name given him on adoption) was on board. In a short time the chief came down to meet his son, bringing with him all his family.

This venerable old chief, Oolooteka, had not seen less than sixty-five years, and yet he measured full six feet in height, and indicated no symptom of the feebleness of age. He had the most courtly carriage in the world, and never a prince sat on a throne with more peerless grace than he presided at the council fire of his people. His wigwam was large and comfortable, and he lived in patriarchal simplicity and abundance. He had ten or twelve servants, a large plantation, and not less than five hundred head of cattle. The wigwam of this aged chieftain was always open to visitors, and his bountiful board was always surrounded by welcome guests. He never slaughtered less than one beef a week throughout the year for his table—a tax on royalty, in a country, too, where no tithes are paid.

Such was the home Houston found waiting for him in the forests. The old chief threw his arms around him, and embraced him with great affection. "My son," said he, "eleven winters have passed since we met. My heart has wondered often where you were; and I heard you were a great chief among your people. Since we parted at the Falls, as you went up the river, I have heard that a dark cloud had fallen on the white path you were walking, and when it fell in your way, you turned your thoughts to my wigwam. I am glad of it—it was done by the Great Spirit. There are many wise men among your people, and they have many councilors in your nation. We are in trouble and the Great Spirit has sent you to us to give us council, and take trouble away from us. I know you will be our friend, for our hearts are near to you, and you will tell our sorrows to the great father, General Jackson. My wigwam is yours—my home is yours—my people are yours—rest with us."

Such was the touching greeting the old chieftain gave him; and Houston has often been heard to say, that when he laid himself down to sleep that night, after the gloom and the sorrows of the last few weeks, he felt like a weary wanderer returned at last to his father's house.

Houston now passed nearly three years among the Cherokees. His history during this period is filled with stirring and beautiful incidents, many of which have come to our knowledge, well worthy of being related, since they would afford the finest pictures of the lights and shadows of forest life. But they would only illustrate more fully those characteristics of stern courage and wild heroism for which he has, throughout his life, been so distinguished, and of which the world will require no better proofs than he has already given. We shall, therefore, pass by the romance of his forest life, at this period, and speak only of his untiring and magnanimous efforts and sacrifices for several years, in behalf of the oppressed and outraged Indians.

The red man on this continent has had few better friends than Houston. From his youth he loved the children of the forest, and among their wigwams had around their council fires he studied the mysteries of their nature. He has declared that, during an intercourse with them of many years, he never was betrayed or deceived by a red man. Long familiarity with them had made him acquainted with their wrongs and their sufferings, and he knew why they looked upon the white man as their foe. He had robbed them of their forests and game— he had laid waste to their wigwams and introduced discord at their council fires—he had, with the glittering bribe of gold and rifles, enticed them away from their ancient haunts, and even driven them at the point of the bayonet from the graves of their fathers—and, worse than all, he had brought among them his accursed *fire-water*, which had melted down the lofty chivalry and unbending strength of their primitive nature, and by that infernal agency degraded and enfeebled a power which, without it, they could never have subdued. This was the forerunner and the hand-maid of his conquests—this was the magic wand he had raised over their stern chieftains, and they had melted away. Was it any wonder that the stricken few who were left of those bold, untameable tribes, that once possessed the fair lands of this broad continent, should know any other feelings towards their usurpers than revenge! Houston knew all their wrongs, and sympathized in all their sufferings. He was now determined to devote himself to their interests, and be the guardian of their rights. He knew that General Jackson, who was then president, felt towards him the affection and confidence of an old and tried friend, and he was resolved to scrutinize the actions of the Indian agents and sub-agents with the greatest severity, and report the result of his observations to the President.

He was always invited to mingle in the councils of the Cherokees during his residence among them, but while he often met them as a friend, he never entered their councils or joined in their deliberations. The Chief counseled with him, often about his people, nor was he long in becoming acquainted with the oppressions and glaring injustice which had been inflicted on them by the agents to whom their affairs had been entrusted in their migration to that country. In exchange for the territory they had occupied lower down on the Arkansas, they were by treaty to receive twenty-eight dollars per capita, which amounted in the aggregate to a vast sum. Instead of paying this money as they should have done, certificates were issued by the agents, under the pretense they had no money, and as paper is always considered worthless by the Indians, merchants who had connections with the agents purchased up these certificates in a fraudulent manner for a mere song, representing that it was very uncertain whether the government ever could send them money. A Mackinaw blanket, a flask of powder, and even a bottle of whiskey, was often all these defrauded exiles ever got for the plighted faith of our government.

In this manner, whole tribes were preyed upon by abandoned speculators, and so completely despoiled of the munificent appropriations of Congress, that it is more than doubtful if a fifth part of the money, secured to them by solemn treaty, ever got into their hands; and even the fraction which went to them only proved a curse. In speaking on this subject, General Houston once said:—

> During the period of my residence among the Indians; in the Arkansas region, I had every facility for gaining a complete knowledge of the flagrant outrages practiced upon the poor Red men by the agents of the government. I saw, every year, vast sums squandered and consumed without the Indians deriving the least benefit,and the government, in very many instances, utterly ignorant of the wrongs that were perpetrated. Had one-third of the money advanced by the government been usefully, honorably, and wisely applied, all those tribes might have been now in possession of the arts and the enjoyments of civilization. I care not what dreamers, and politicians, and travelers, and writers say to the contrary, I know the Indian character, and I confidently avow, that if one-third of the many millions of dollars our government has appropriated within the last twenty-five years, for the benefit of the Indian population, had been honestly and judiciously applied, there would not have been at this time a single tribe within the limits of our States and Territories, but what would have been in the complete enjoyment of all the arts and all the comforts of civilized life. But there is not a tribe but has been outraged and defrauded; and nearly all the wars we have prosecuted against the Indians, have grown out of the bold frauds and the cruel injustice played off upon them by our Indian agents and their accomplices. But the purposes for which these vast annuities and enormous contingent advances were made have

only led to the destructor of the constitutions of thousands and the increase of immorality among the Indians. We cannot measure the desolating effects of intoxicating liquors among the Indians by any analogy drawn from civilized life. With the Red man the consequences are a thousand times more frightful. Strong drink, when once introduced among the Indians, unnerves the purposes of the good, and gives energy to the passions of the vicious; it saps the constitution with fearful rapidity, and inflames all the ferocity of the savage nature. The remoteness of their situation excludes them from all the benefits that might arise from a thorough knowledge of their condition by the President, who only hears one side of the story, and that, too, told by his own creatures, whose motives in seeking for such stations are often only to be able to gratify their cupidity and avarice. The President should be careful to whom Indian agencies are given. If there are trusts under our government where honest and just men are needed, they are needed in such places; where speculation and fraud can be more easily perpetrated than anywhere else. For in the far off forests beyond the Mississippi, where we have exiled these unfortunate tribes, they can perpetrate their crimes and their outrages, and no eye but the Almighty's sees them.

During the entire period he resided in that region, he was unceasing in his efforts to prevent the introduction of ardent spirits among the Indians; and though, for more than a year, he had a trading establishment between the Grand River and the Verdigris, he never introduced or trafficked in those destructive drinks. This, too, was at a period when he was far from being a practically temperate man himself. But, whatever might be his own occasional indulgences during his visits to Fort Gibson and other white settlements, he had too much humanity and love for the Red men, ever to contribute to their crimes or their misfortunes by introducing or trafficking in those damnable poisons.

Cognizant of the frauds practiced on these various tribes by the agents of the government, he could not endure such intolerable acts of outrage upon the rights and the sympathies of those whom he could not but esteem a generous and a good people; and he determined their conduct should be known at the seat of government, not doubting they would be instantly removed. He visited Washington early in 1832, and made such representations as caused an investigation into their conduct, and not less than five agents and sub-agents were promptly removed.

These disgraced men were, some of them, *highly respectable*, and they had powerful friends in Congress. Their dismissal from office was, therefore, the signal for a general attack upon Houston from every quarter, where mortified pride or disappointed cupidity was aroused; and even to this day these attacks are made. Before leaving Arkansas, the swindlers, whose conduct he had exposed, had crowded the journals of that region with the basest and most infamous libels against Houston's character. He had been the friend of the despoiled Red Man, and when he saw a band of land pirates leagued together to rob the poor Indian, his humanity was stirred, and he fearlessly tore off the mask which covered these perpetrators of such high-handed injustice. But it was a crime for which they never forgave him—and all that money, lavishly used, and friends in high stations, who shared the spoils of the robbers and a venal press, all moved by untiring malignity, could accomplish, to cover Houston with infamy—*was done*.

At that time, hostility against General Jackson had reached its culminating point. There was a majority against him in Congress, and this majority were bent upon his ruin as a public man. All the agencies that are resorted to, to crush a great man who is rising into fame, had been tried. Calumny had exhausted its venom, and hatred had belched forth all its malignity. But the heroic old man had gone through it all unscathed, and he now sat calm and high above the shafts of his foes.

But Houston was the sworn friend of the old General, and being a young man, he could be more easily crushed. A desperate effort was made to rally against him all the foes of General Jackson, and the effort was successful. One charge which he had made against the agents, and proved incontrovertibly, seemed to multiply their former malignity a hundred fold. They had been contractors for furnishing Indian rations; and through their injustice or delinquency, some of the Indians had died of starvation, and to multitudes only a scanty and insufficient supply of food had been issued. These rations were issued at but one point in the two Nations (Creeks and Cherokees), which compelled the emigrants, as they had not had the benefit of a crop, to locate in the most unhealthy parts of the country, for there only their rations could be obtained. This prevented their establishment and creation of homes in the new country, to which they had emigrated.

When the mask was torn off from this den of iniquity, by the bold, humane hand of Houston, he was attacked and pursued with ferocious malignity.

But it was not enough to have stirred up the press of the nation against a lofty-minded and upright man: Now, all Congress was to be moved against him. It was necessary, in this last desperate crusade, to hit upon a file-leader, who had distinguished himself for his malignant, personal hatred of General Jackson, and, at the same time, he must have no scruples against being the supple tool of wiser, but not better men, who pulled the wires behind the scenes. Characters of this description were not wanting in the Congress that waged this THIRD PUNIC WAR against the old Man of the Hermitage; but the most supple, brazen-faced, shameless of all, was a certain politician, who had been elected as a friend of Jackson. He was chosen as the best instrument they could find to use for their purposes. In his place in the House of Representatives, he assailed Houston, and charged him with an attempt to obtain a fraudulent contract for Indian Rations, and he boldly intimated that the Secretary of War, and even General Jackson himself, were implicated in the attempt to defraud!

A crisis had now come. Houston had suffered all sorts of abuse before, and borne it in silence, but when he saw the fame, and even the integrity of Gen. Jackson, ruthlessly assailed *on his account*, by a member of Congress, he was determined to chastise him for his cowardly insolence to the President. He knew Houston's determination, and was careful not to cross his path. At last, one evening, when he knew, by positive information, that Houston was *not armed*, he crossed over to the other side of Pennsylvania Avenue (where Houston was walking) for the purpose of perpetrating some foul deed in the dark, we have a right to suppose, since it was proved on the trial that he was armed, and did attempt the life of Houston, who had no weapon about him but a hickory cane.

As soon as Houston recognized his antagonist, through the moonlight, he asked him if he name was _____ of Ohio. The answer had no sooner escaped his lips, than Houston, who knew he had no time to lose, since he was unarmed, leveled him to the ground, and shivered his hickory cane upon his head. In the meantime, he had snapped a pistol at Houston, but it missed fire, or he had been a dead man, for it was held to his breast. Houston spared his life, and the politician crawled off to his bed, which he kept some days.

The chastised member now caused four processes to be commenced against Houston, by which he expected to crush and disgrace him forever. He was arrested by the Sergeant-at-arms, and brought before the House of Representatives, who resolved themselves into a judicial tribunal, to try him on the charge of violation of the rights of one of their members, whom Houston had held responsible for words uttered in debate. The court sat nearly thirty days, and no means were spared to condemn the accused man. It was argued, and with great ability, by his friends, that the House had no jurisdiction in the case; that by the Constitution, Congress had been made a legislative assembly, but clothed with no judicial powers over American citizens. In this opinion, too, it is but just to add, some of Gen. Jackson's political opponents concurred. The matter dragged on nearly a month, and as the conduct, the character, and the winning personal appearance of Houston were continually gaining him friends, and the public were becoming indignant that Congress should abandon the business of the country to prosecute and lacerate an unfortunate and self-exiled man, who had bled in its service; even his foes themselves became tired of the prosecution. On the trial, Houston spoke in his own defense, at great length, and with consummate eloquence and ability. It was a touching spectacle, to see a man who had been four years a member of that body, the governor of a great State, the bosom friend of Gen. Jackson, one who bore on his body the deep wounds received in fighting under the flag waving from the top of the Capitol, arraigned by party politicians before their bar, for having, in protecting himself, while unarmed, from the stealthy attack of an armed coward, chastised a renegade demagogue, who had dared to charge the President of the United States with a bold fraud, because he thought he could, in his place in Congress, do it with impunity. Politicians of a certain class will at last learn, that in their attempts *to crush* those bold and magnanimous men who stand by the masses of the people, and have, from the very beginning of the government, led the popular majorities—they are only hastening their advancement to power.

What turned the popular feeling in favor of Houston at the time, and made him dear to the people, just in proportion as he was persecuted, was the undeniable fact that he was brought to the rack and tortured there, *because of his enthusiastic love for his old General, who was then President.*

This protracted and august trial ended in a party vote of instructions to the Speaker, to reprimand the prisoner at the bar of the House. But the reprimand was delivered in so courteous and delicate a manner, it carried with it more of the tone of an approval than a reprimand. It was everywhere regarded as a signal triumph to Houston, for few men ever had so mighty a power marshaled against them.

The second process was to move for a committee to be appointed to investigate the truth of the charge that member had made against Houston, of fraud in procuring a contract for furnishing Indian rations. A committee was raised and *the demagogue was appointed chairman*, which threw into his hands power to crush his enemy, if the fraud could be proved. Houston, conscious of his innocence, had procured this measure to be adopted himself. And what was the result of this second attempt to ruin this man, who had come from his distant exile only on the humane mission—which an angel might have undertaken—of procuring justice for the outraged Indians? After a tedious and thorough investigation—after marshaling every circumstance they could to his prejudice, the committee was *compelled to report that not the slightest evidence had appeared to sustain the charge.*

Houston was still triumphant, and his foes made *another* effort. They introduced a resolution to exclude him forever from the lobby of the House, where, as an ex-Member of Congress, and the governor of a state, he had a right to go. But this also failed!

Every process that could either injure or disgrace him had now been tried in Congress, and so far from crushing him, he had been steadily rising. The *fourth* and last act in this disgraceful drama then opened. At the instance of this same demagogue, who, by being flogged by Houston, had now won, what was doubtless to him, a very gratifying notoriety, he was indicted and held to bail in a criminal process of $20,000. He could have evaded the trial by leaving the District, but he met his enemy once more, and after twenty days he was fined $500 and costs. But no enforcement of the sentence of the court was ever attempted. It is worthy of remark, that the last act but one of General Jackson's administration was to remit the fine.

Seldom, if ever, in the history of this country, has so malignant a persecution been waged against a public man. Seldom, in the history of the world, has a man been able to withstand so mighty a conspiracy. But Houston came off triumphantly. During this entire period of attack and abuse he had displayed no cowardice nor shunned the most searching scrutiny. He had bared his breast to his foes, and invited their weapons. And now, when they had given over the contest, and retired from it loaded with mortification and contempt, this hunted and persecuted man deliberately abandoned once more the haunts of civilization, and went voluntarily where his foes never could have driven him—back to his exile.

He returned by the way of Tennessee, and wherever he went he was received with every demonstration of regard. Years had passed since other painful occurrences had taken place—and with them had passed, too, the storm they had raised. Reason had resumed its sway over the public mind, and a strong desire was manifested that he should again take up his abode in Tennessee. The recent persecutions he had just passed through had only won for him a deeper sympathy than ever, and all the pride of the state was aroused to protect and honor the man it had lost. But he could not be dissuaded from his purpose of returning once more to the forest. A sight of the spot where he had seen the bright hopes that had greeted his early manhood, crushed in a single hour, only awakened associations he wished to forget; and he once more turned his face towards the distant wigwam of the old Indian Chief, where, after a year of persecution from Christian man, he found repose by the hearthstone of a savage king—a biting satire upon civilized life. It is not difficult to imagine the effect that such unrelenting persecution must have produced upon a sensitive, a proud and a magnanimous man. He had escaped civilized life, and gone where its pestiferous and calumny-loaded breath could not reach him. He had no more ambition to gratify. Posts of honor and emolument proffered by General Jackson, he rejected, for he would never suffer the foes of the old warrior and statesman to heap opprobrium upon his name for showing favor to a proscribed man.

CHAPTER VI:
TEXAS—THE NEW FIELD

His intention was now to become a herdsman, and spend the rest of his life in the tranquility of the prairie solitudes. A fondness for rural pursuits was now the only passion he had to gratify. Leaving his wigwam, which was situated on the margin of a prairie between the Verdigris and the Grand River, a short distance from its junction with the Arkansas, he set out on the 1st of December, 1832, with a few companions, through the wilderness to Fort Towson. At Nacogdoches he reported himself to the authorities, and a few days after went on to San Felipe de Austin, the seat of government of Austin's Colony; after reporting to the authorities, he prosecuted his journey to San Antonio de Bexar.

Here he held an interview with a delegation of the Comanche Indians on a visit to that place. In all his intercourse with the authorities and citizens, his conduct was marked by great respect for law and the institutions of the country. After some days he returned with two companions to San Felipe de Austin. At Nacogdoches he was now warmly solicited to establish his permanent residence, and allow his name to be used as candidate for election to a convention which was to meet in the following April. (In view of the probable necessity of revolutionizing Texas, the people of the country openly and generally expressed themselves in favor of inviting either Houston or Carroll to come among them, and head any revolutionary movement that might be determined on.)

He was slow now to yield to their request, for his purpose had been formally settled to abandon public life and enjoy the repose and solitude of a forest home. But a single glance at the resources of this new country, and the character and condition of its population, satisfied him that a great destiny awaited them, and in imagination he already saw a new commonwealth rising into power. He was still, in the morning of life—here was a new field for achievement, where all the bold elements of his character could find full play. Once embarked on the stream of a revolution the world would learn, at last, the character of the man it had hunted from society, and history and time would pronounce his eulogy. Sober reflection convinced him that his public life was hardly yet begun, and he permitted them to use his name for the suffrages of the people, who seemed at once to recognize his great qualities as a civil and military leader.

While the election was going on he returned to Natchitoches, in Louisiana, and made a report to the government of the United States. Its origin is supposed to have been in the fact of his having been requested by General Jackson to ascertain the disposition of the Comanches to make peace with our government, and to prevail upon a delegation of that numerous and warlike nation to visit Fort Gibson on the Arkansas, and afterwards proceed to Washington. General Jackson thought that the emigration of the Choctaws, the Chickasaws, and the Creeks, would be promoted by a treaty of peace with the Comanches, whose power and hostile disposition they dreaded in establishing themselves in their new home. As this was a confidential mission, little is known of its history. But it is certain that in Houston's interview with the Comanches at Bexar, the objects were accomplished which had been contemplated by the mission.

On his return to Nacogdoches he learned that during his absence he had been elected by a unanimous vote. He took up his residence among his new constituents, who had extended towards him so generous a greeting.

This convention, which was composed of more than fifty members, assembled at San Felipe de Austin, the first of April, 1833. It was the first deliberate assembly, made up of men descended from the Anglo-Saxon race, which had ever assembled within the limits of the ancient dominions of Cortez, and the first step in that stupendous movement, which has already swept across the Cordillera Mountains to the green shores of the Pacific, where a thousand young riflemen from New York and New England are going to plant fortresses of protection, and institutions of learning, like those which are now over-shadowing the crumbling despotisms of two hemispheres.

The convention met in a rude, narrow apartment—as the first colonists of the Grecian states are said to have organized those matchless republics of antiquity, under rude tents in the forests, robed in the skins of wild beasts. But there were men there, whose deliberations involved the fate of many millions.

As the delegates had their own expenses to pay, they proceeded forthwith to the business which had called them together, and in thirteen days, they completed one of the best models extant for a state constitution. It was signed by the members, and a memorial adopted by the Convention: Stephen F. Austin, William H. Wharton, President of the Convention, and James B. Miller, were appointed commissioners to bear the constitution and memorial to the supreme government of Mexico, and obtain the recognition of Texas as one of the states of the confederacy. The memorial set forth various reasons why Texas should become one of the states of Mexico; amongst others, that it would enable her to negotiate terms with the hostile Indian tribes, and secure their rights to land previously promised by the general government. Encroachments had been made on the Indian territory, subsequent to the rupture between the colonists and the Mexican soldiers, stationed at Nacogdoches, Velasco and Anahuac. This rupture had taken place in the summer of 1832, in consequence of a difference between Bustamente and Santa Anna. The former had attempted to subvert the constitution of 1824, and the military throughout Texas had pronounced in his favor. Santa Anna declared himself the friend and supporter of the constitution, and the colonists siding with him in the civil revolution, which had begun in Mexico and spread to Texas, had expelled the military, whose usurpations, up to that time, had been submitted to without murmuring. Santa Anna was now in power, and the colonists doubted not that Austin and his colleagues would be received with favor, and their constitution ratified by the Federal authorities.

Austin alone finally went to the city of Mexico. He was received with some formality, but little encouragement was given to his mission. *In the meantime Santa Anna had resolved on establishing a military despotism, which was the only reason that could have been urged against accepting the constitution.*

In the formation of that instrument the greatest care had been taken to render it entirely acceptable to the Central Government. In the organization of the States of Mexico, under the Federal Constitution of 1824, the Provinces of Texas and Coahuila formed one state, but the right had been reserved to Texas of constituting herself a distinct state when her population would justify the measure. The Federal Government and Coahuila had for some time pursued towards Texas a policy which rendered it necessary for her to become a separate state as soon as possible. They had granted away her territory in large tracts, under the pretense of raising funds to enable Mexico to defend her frontiers against the Indians, but she had never appropriated one dollar to that object. For, whenever the Central Administration stationed any troops in Texas, it was in the towns nearest to the seaboard, where no hostile attack from the savages could be apprehended. Here, with a military force to overawe the citizens, a support of the government, which would never otherwise have been conceded, could be extorted. The frontiers were left without protection, and the colonists were obliged to protect themselves as best they could, against the hostile incursions of fifteen or twenty tribes of Indians.

We have already said that great care was taken to render the new constitution acceptable to the Federal Government. Mexico, for example, had no banks. In the Convention a measure had been brought forward, and an article proposed to be inserted, authorizing the legislature of the State of Texas to create a bank or banks. This measure was introduced by Branch T. Archer, and supported by the principal men in the Convention. Houston was the only speaker who opposed the policy. In principle he was opposed to any system of banking, except one whose powers could be brought within very narrow limits; and he did not believe a more fatal precedent could be established in the infancy of the new state. The exigencies of cupidity and of business would prove stronger than the enactments of law, and he was persuaded that no sound system of banking could be hoped for in so new a community.

But he was opposed to the measure also, on the ground of policy. It would be a valid reason, if inserted, for Mexico to reject the constitution, since it would be an innovation upon the legislation of the general government, and he was deeply anxious to preserve harmony, and wished Texas to defer to the prejudices and institutions of Mexico, rather than excite her jealousy by any of these new movements, which would at least be likely to excite suspicion, if not positive alarm. Houston spoke on this subject with great eloquence and convincing power. He caused the article in dispute to be stricken out, and one inserted prohibiting the establishment of all banks and banking corporations, for a period of ninety-nine years, which passed the Convention by a large majority.

This was the first illustration Houston gave, of that wise and profound policy, which guided all his counsels during the long struggle Texas was obliged to pass, before she could be admitted to the full and recognized liberties of an American commonwealth. We shall often have occasion to remark the difference between his policy, and that of other public men, who figured on the same scene. All new states are infested, more or less, by a class of busy, noisy, second-rate men, who are always in favor of rash and extreme measures. But Texas was absolutely overrun by such men. There seemed to be few of that class who give character to the institutions of new states, which spring suddenly into power—men who are brave enough for any trial of courage, wise enough for any difficult emergency, and cool enough for any crisis of danger. But fortunately, Texas had some such men, and she had a leader she depended on in the camp, and a councilor she relied on in the Senate. It is exceedingly doubtful what would have been her fate, but for him. And yet, we shall perceive, as we trace down Houston's history, involving, as it necessarily docs, the history of Texas, that all his difficulties and all the dangers of the state, and the sufferings and sacrifices of her people, grew out of the rash and headstrong movements of a few men, whose judgments and counsels were generally precipitate, and ended, when followed, in embarrassing the state or plunging her into danger.

Those who were present in the Convention, have always attributed to Houston the moulding influence which controlled the action of that assembly, which gave tone to the political feelings and events that followed. They are also just as confident in the belief, that if restless and ambitious spirits, who will "rule or rend," had been willing to follow Houston's wise counsels, the independence of Texas would have been achieved without much sacrifice of blood or treasure. We shall see how he at last triumphed, and how much sacrifice, and care, and endurance, it cost him and his country.

But to return to Austin, whom we left in Mexico, and in trouble. Finding his application failed, he concluded to return to Texas. On his way home, he was pursued by order of the government, taken back to the capital, and plunged into a dungeon, where he dragged out many months of gloom and suffering. He was an amiable, enlightened, excellent man, and a pure patriot. He was beloved and respected by the colonists, and his fame and his virtues will be long cherished by the Texians. During his imprisonment, stories of his sufferings reached Texas, and everywhere produced a deep sensation. The indignation of the colonists burst forth like the rage of a single man.

There was, at that time, only one press, in Texas (at Brazoria), but it gave utterance to the wrongs of the people; and although few in numbers (for the entire population of Texas did not exceed 20,000 souls), yet, instead of exercising discretion, they spoke freely of the wrongs they endured, and the rights guaranteed to them under the Constitution of 1824. Houston discouraged such unrestrained ebullitions of feeling, since they would be likely to plunge Texas into a bloody struggle with Mexico *before she was prepared for it,* while he was as anxious as any man for the day of their political redemption to come.

Austin had been cast into prison with no formal accusation alleged against him, and without even the form of a trial. At length he was liberated by Santa Anna, and permitted to return home. He had great confidence in Austin, for he had shown himself a friend of order on all occasions in Texas, and loyal to the principles recognized at the time. He had first migrated to that country with 300 families, as colonists, and thus introduced the materials of that vast political structure, which was subsequently wrought into form and beauty. When he returned to Texas, he found the public mind inflamed, and indignation had been expressed in municipal meetings. But when public feeling was subsiding, and few, if any, orderly men were thinking of extreme measures, Santa Anna showed clearly that nothing short of absolute power would satisfy him.

The colonists were alarmed, and precautionary measures taken. They were ruled by Mexican laws, and governed by officers who followed blindly Mexican edicts. Rumors were constantly reaching Texas, that the colonists were laboring under the disapprobation of the Mexican government. The commerce of Texas had been placed under restrictions of the most oppressive character, and the worst men had been set over the administration of the customs. Taxation had become oppressive. The people had been baffled in all their attempts to secure justice, and large sums of money extorted from them in obtaining titles to the lands they had improved, and which had been guaranteed to them by the Mexican government. An edict of Santa Anna had demanded of the people the surrender of their private arms. This struck them like an *electric shock*. It not only exposed their wives and children to the fury of hostile Indians, but to all the horrors of starvation, for many families depended upon wild game for daily subsistence.

At Gonzales, there was a piece of artillery for the defense of the place, which was called into almost weekly requisition by the incursions of the Indians. It was the capital of Dewitt's Colony, situated on the eastern bank of the Guadalupe, about 70 miles east of Bexar. In obedience to Santa Anna's edict, Ugartechea, a Colonel in the Mexican army, in command of several hundred dragoons, marched to Gonzales, from Bexar, to carry off the four pounder. The colonists flocked together for the rescue of the little field-piece. Some skirmishing took place, without any serious consequences at the moment. But a great point had been won—*the first shot had been fired by the Mexican army*, and the swords drawn that day, were to be returned no more to their scabbards, till the last link in the Mexican fetters which had been put on the youthful form of Texan Liberty, had been snapped asunder, and she stood erect among the nations.

Austin arrived at the scene of the struggle, and was elected General of the forces. But the insurgents not only rescued their four pounder, they resolved to pursue the enemy to Bexar, and drive the base myrmidons of the Mexican tyrant from their soil. A general alarm was spread to the banks of the Sabine. Eastern Texas had hitherto been disposed to remain tranquil, supposing all might not be so bad as rumor proclaimed it;—but the torch of war had now been lighted, and Texas rose everywhere like a single man.

Committees of Vigilance and of Safety had been constituted in the municipalities of San Augustine and Nacogdoches, and a partial organization of the militia under their direction had taken place. In the meantime, Houston had been chosen General of Texas, east of the Trinity. An invitation had been given by the people of the county of Brazoria, and responded to by other municipalities to elect delegates to meet in a general consultation to devise means of safety, in the event of danger; for they had now become pretty well satisfied that they had little to hope for from the despot of Mexico.

Austin had proceeded on to Bexar with his forces, and invested. The colonists marched to him from all sections of the province, till 800 armed men has joined his standard. These events occurred in October, 1835. The Consultation was to meet early in that month at Washington, and at the specified time about fifty-six delegates assembled. At their first meeting they conferred, and changed the place of deliberation to San Felipe, where they received an invitation from General Austin to repair to Bexar, pledging himself, if they complied, that he would reduce the place in three days. After his advance upon Bexar, citizens residing near Matagorda and Victoria formed a company, and under the command of Captain Collinsworth, reduced Goliad, and maintained possession of the town. On the first meeting of the Consultation, General Austin wrote to Houston to send on his division of troops. Houston took from his pocket the last five dollars he had in the world, and put it into the hand of a good rider, with dispatches to his division, and in a short time the Redlanders were rapidly mustering for the scene of war. Immediately after having received the invitation of General Austin, Houston, with the major part of the Consultation, set out without delay for Austin's camp, at the Salado, within three miles of Bexar.

Soon after their arrival, General Austin, in whose pure and lofty mind love of country outweighed all considerations of personal aggrandizement, feeling diffident to lead an army at such a time, proposed to surrender his command to Houston. Houston most positively declined his magnanimous offer, alleging, among other reasons, that the troops then in the field were either those who had elected Austin as their commander or had marched to the camp in obedience to his requisition, and he believed it would furnish a pretext for the seditious and disaffected to abandon the service, and defeat the objects of the campaign. But he frankly offered to render General Austin any aid in his power in organizing or drilling his command. A Council of War was held in the camp, to which the principal officers and members of the Consultation were invited. A question arose as to the propriety, or rather necessity, of forming a provisional government, which could be done only by the re-assembling of the members of the Consultation at San Felipe. In this exigency the Council of War determined to refer the subject to the army. The following day the troops were drawn up and their voice taken. They were unanimous in the opinion that the Consultation ought to reassemble and form a provisional government, and devise ways and means for maintaining the army then in the field, and adopt such measures as would give Texas credit abroad.

After General Austin had marched the army some ten or twelve miles below to the Mission of Espada, the members of the Consultation repaired to San Felipe, where they reorganized, and once more opened their deliberations. They made a provisional declaration, exhorting all Mexicans to unite in maintaining the Constitution of 1824, and pledged their lives, property, and sacred honor, in support of its principles. They established an organic law for the provisional government of the province, and organized a temporary administration for it. Houston was one of the committee to frame the declaration. A disposition existed on the part of the members of the committee to make a declaration of absolute independence, and such a resolution was adopted. Considering this movement premature and ill-judged, he got a member of the majority to move for a reconsideration of the vote. By one of the ablest efforts of his life, he carried his point, and on the trial there was found to be a considerable majority in favor of the *Provisional* Declaration.

These deliberations were held in a little framed building of one floor, without ceiling or plaster, whose only apartment was the narrow room where they assembled. Houston, as was his custom in those days, was dressed in buckskin breeches, and a Mexican blanket. But the appearance of the room, and the costume of the members, had little to do with their deliberations. In regard to this freak of Houston, of dressing for years *a la sauvage*, General Jackson is reported to have said, he "thanked God there was one man, at least, in Texas whom the Almighty had had the making of, and not the tailor." When Houston took up his abode in the forests, he assumed the simple and picturesque costume of the proud race among whom he dwelt; that portion of the world, which had poured gall into his lacerated bosom, and finally hunted him into the forests, now invaded the solitude of his new home. One of his crimes was that he had become an Indian—even in his dress. Certainly these men "the tailors had had the making of"—and he must have been an outlaw, whose dress was more like a Roman senator's than the dandy of the *Boulevards*.

Some of Napoleon's officers were once laughing, on the morning of one of his great battles, at the gay dress of Murat as he rode by, decked in ribbons and plumes. "You may smile, Messieurs," said Napoleon, "at my dandy marshal, but take care that when the columns are shot down today, you keep your eye upon him, for where you see Murat's gaudy plumes they will be dancing in the hottest of the fight. Let a hero have one folly, gentlemen." Diogenes lived in a tub, but from all accounts the world felt a good deal more disturbed about it than the old philosopher himself.

Yes, Houston, the adopted son of an Indian chief, wore the dress of his tribe, but he carried the heart of a hero under his blanket. He refused to be a candidate for any office; what he could do, however, he was ready to do. A governor and lieutenant-governor were elected. A council was also created, one member from each municipality, and the requisite number of officers appointed for the administration of such a government. The council was to continue in session till they should be superseded by officers elected by the people. Measure, were also taken for raising a regular army and organizing the militia.

Another event took place which decided the fate of Texas. The man in buckskin and the Mexican blanket was, with only one dissenting voice among more than fifty members, elected COMMANDER-IN-CHIEF OF THE ARMIES OF TEXAS.

There was no alternative for Houston but to accept the office. There was no one else gifted with those great qualities nature lavishes on men born to command. He accepted the appointment, and proceeded to appoint his staff, and draw up the necessary bills for the organization of the army, and the appointment of the officers of the line, embracing a competent organization of the forces designed to be raised.

Texas had not a dollar at this time, and previous to Houston's election, commissioners had been appointed to visit the United States to forward her interests, and procure a loan to sustain her under the pressure of her bold undertaking. Austin, Wharton, and Archer were appointed commissioners, and they were already on their way. Houston's hopes of money were not sanguine. He regarded Texas as thrown upon her own resources, and such aids as could be afforded by individuals whom the spirit of patriotism should inspire with generosity. At that moment, there were few men in the United States who had any adequate conception of the importance of those early movements, or dreamed of the results that were to follow. Even now, as these grand events of the last ten years pass in review before us, we seem, in the soberness of solitary reflection, to be tracing the progress of one of the states of antiquity. But there are few men who understand great social or political changes till they have become matters of history. We shall, in the sequel, glance at some of the causes which have operated to cloud and prejudice the minds of the people of this country on the entire subject of Texas.

In the meantime, General Houston issued a proclamation inviting five thousand volunteers to unite in the cause of Texas. The army still remained in the field under Burleson, who had succeeded to the command after General Austin had left for the United States. He was an early settler of Texas, and a good man, but destitute of those great qualities which fit men for military control. Before General Austin left the army, Fannin and Bowie, with about one hundred men, encountered five hundred Mexicans at the Mission Concepción. The action was sustained gallantly by the Americans, and the Mexicans retreated, leaving some dead on the field, and carrying with them many wounded. The victors then marched to the neighborhood of Bexar, and posted themselves above the town. Colonel Benj. R. Milam, who had then no command in the army, proposed that volunteers should turn out, who were willing to enter the town of Bexar and storm the place. About two hundred flocked to his banner, and led by the gallant Milam, whose chivalry entitled him to the confidence of such brave men, entered the town at night, and taking possession of certain buildings, made their way with crowbars through the walls, from house to house. After performing acts of singular bravery for several days, the heroic Milam fell, his head pierced by a rifle-ball; and shortly after their leader's death, the troops got entire possession of the town, and the Alamo (the enemy's fortress) capitulated.

A singular spectacle was presented on the morning of the capitulation. Not less than eleven hundred Mexican soldiers passed before a little band of less than two hundred Texians, and laid down their arms. They were released on their parole of honor, and marched to Mexico by General Cos. This same general violated his faith, and fought at San Jacinto. The colonists were now generally discharged, and marched to their homes, with the exception of the gallant company which had reduced the Alamo. During the siege of Bexar, a company called the New Orleans Greys, under Captain Morris, and another company from Mobile, under Captain Breeze, had arrived, as volunteers from the United States. They bore a gallant part in the siege, and every man engaged in the town deserved and secured the renown of a hero.

While the troops were before Bexar, a Doctor Grant arrived, and joined the army. He had been concerned with an English mining company at Parras, but he had fallen under the displeasure of the Mexican government, and was obliged to fly. He was a Scotsman by birth, but did not seem to possess much of the methodical shrewdness which characterizes that nation. He was a man of much more than ordinary capacity, but, in all military affairs, seemed to be destitute of judgment and discretion. As one of the aids of General Austin, he claimed the command of the troops remaining, after Burleson had retired with most of the army. He immediately projected the invasion of Matamoros, for he entertained a single-hearted hatred of the Mexicans, and he induced the New Orleans Greys and Capt. Breeze's company from Mobile to join him in the expedition. These two companies accordingly took up their march for Matamoros by the way of Goliad. At the same time Grant opened a correspondence with the General Council, which unfortunately at the time contained some men of capacity utterly destitute of moral principle, and carrying on machinations which were in the end to terminate most disastrously for Texas. The members of the Military Committee of the General Council coincided with Grant's plan of attack upon Matamoros, and thought it necessary, in effecting its capture, to destroy Houston's influence, and create a power that would supersede him.

In the appointment of his staff, General Houston had chosen J. W. Fannin, Jr., his Inspector General. He had had command at the battle of the Mission Concepción, and arriving at the Council of San Felipe, Houston, who felt that he deserved an appointment in the line of the army, obtained for him the colonelcy of the regiment of artillery, which placed him next in command to himself.

The Council, to effect their designs without reference to the safety of the country, thought proper to direct the headquarters of the army to be established at Washington, about fifty miles distant from the sessions of the Council. This, of necessity, removed Houston's station, and it was evident they believed the success of their intrigues depended upon getting him as far off as possible. About the middle of December he repaired to Washington, and continued there, engaged in his arduous duties. Meantime he had assigned the officers of the regular army to their several recruiting stations, and directed them to make such reports as would enable him, at any time, to know the amount and condition of the regular force.

Fannin was ordered to Brazoria, the principal recruiting rendezvous, and Houston supposed, of course, that his orders would be carried out with a strict regard to his authority. But his dispatches were utterly disregarded. About this time, letters were circulated through the country to create a suspicion that Houston's design was to establish a military government by raising five thousand volunteers, through the sanction of the General Council.

Houston bore this in silence, but endeavored to counteract it by the efficiency of his conduct. About the 1st of January he received orders from Governor Smith,—who had detected the secret intrigues of the Council with Grant, Fannin and others—to repair to San Felipe, while the general had been at Washington. Colonel Ward's command from Georgia, and the Alabamians, had arrived at the mouth of the Brazos. Houston had taken precautions, and issued his orders for all troops that might arrive in the country, requiring them to report to the governor as nominal commander-in-chief, and to himself as commander of the army, on their arrival. Fannin being in the neighborhood of the United States volunteers when they landed, paid no attention to the orders of General Houston, and abandoning his post as an officer of the regular army, became a candidate for the colonelcy of the regiment that was to be formed by the union of the Georgia and Alabama troops. Governor Smith no sooner detected the treasonable conspiracy of the Council, than he manifested the highest disapprobation of their conduct, and of course excited their hottest displeasure. Fannin treated all General Houston's dispatches with cool contempt, and looked only to the orders of the Council. He had made known to them his desire to be elected colonel of the new regiment, and in accordance with their views, he was chosen to the new post, Ward being put second in command. They were then ordered to sail from Velasco to Copano, and thence to march to Refugio Mission, twenty miles distant from their landing, where Grant was to join them with his command, on their way to Matamoros.

In obedience to his orders, Houston reported to the governor at San Felipe, and was ordered to repair to Refugio, where a juncture of the troops was to be effected. He returned forthwith to Washington, and after arranging matters at headquarters, proceeded to the execution of the governor's orders. He reached Goliad about the middle of January, 1836, and found Grant and his troops on the eve of departure for Refugio. General Houston made known to the troops the orders under which he was acting, and urged obedience to his authority. Ignorant of the extent to which the Council had gone in thwarting his intentions to save the country by routing the enemy on their first great engagement, and knowing it was impossible for the troops at Bexar to maintain the place, he dispatched Colonels Bowie and Bonham (of South Carolina) on the 15th of January, with an escort to Bexar, directing the commanding officer to blow up the Alamo, and fall back to Gonzales on the Guadalupe, which he intended to make the line of defense.

Grant and Morris refused obedience to the orders of the governor, while Houston was left without the power of accounting for their extraordinary conduct. He marched with them twenty-five miles to Refugio Mission, leaving a few Regulars to maintain the post at Goliad, with no subsistence but the cattle of the country. He arrived at Refugio, but no intelligence had come of Fannin's landing.

The governor, refusing to concur in their lawless measures, had been deposed by the Council, although—under the Organic Law, which required a certain number to constitute the Council, or transact business—they had ceased to be a lawful body. The conduct of the stormy spirits in that Council had disgusted and enraged their more patriotic and rational colleagues,and unwilling to concur in their high-handed and treacherous movements, they had withdrawn, reducing their ambitious associates to an incompetent number. But they were nevertheless determined to brave it out, and "rule or rend."

Houston did not wish to be the cause of insubordination, for he was aware that it would require all the harmony and union possible to save the country. Yet knowing that all the troops from the United States had left with the expectation of serving under himself, he used every persuasive he thought convincing against the expedition to Matamoros, and then resolved to return and report in person to the governor.

The only object of the Council in directing the campaign upon Matamoros, was to command the revenues of the place. Houston at once discovered the absurdity of such a plan, since the possession of Matamoros by an enemy would cut off all intercourse with the interior, and prevent all communication with the sea, and he had forecast enough to know that if an army could reach Matamoros without opposition, they could not maintain it a single week with a force of only seven hundred men. But they could never reach sight of its walls. They had an area of several hundred miles to pass, with no means of transportation—they had not three days of breadstuffs, and the men were unprovided in every respect for a campaign.

Houston remonstrated with the officers in a friendly manner, representing the great difficulties they would have to encounter, the futility of the project, and the disasters attendant on a failure. So careful was he to avoid exciting sedition among the troops, who bowed very reluctantly to the command of any other general, that he set out from Refugio in the night, with a few of his staff, for San Felipe.

On the road he received news that the Council had deposed the governor and superseded his own authority—also, letters of Col. Fannin, which had been published, showing his reliance on the Council, and disregarding all other authorities. This opened Houston's eyes to the true situation of the country, and he saw that unless something was done, without delay, to repair the evil, and to prepare the nation for the trying struggle she must pass, in wading through a Revolution, all would be lost. The hopes, which had greeted the first dawning of Anglo-Saxon liberty in the fair province of New Estramadura, seemed likely to be extinguished; and it is not strange that a man who had been prevailed on to exchange the tranquility of a forest life, where he could find repose from persecution, to mingle in the struggles of a nation emerging into a free existence, should, when he saw himself still hunted down by malignant rivals, and his hopes clouded, feel his great heart dejected by sadness.

But men whom God raises up to become leaders of nations cannot be crushed—and although in the midst of their adversities they may seem, for a moment, to bow before the blast, yet they never despair. For not more sure was Columbus to surmount at last all opposition, and plant his feet upon the green shores of the New World, than are such men in the end to overcome all their foes, and triumph over even the malignity of fortune. All the way to San Felipe, he was halting in the most painful suspense—whether to withdraw once more from the treacheries and persecutions of the world, and bury himself deep in the holy solitudes of nature, and pass a life of communion with the Great Spirit, and his beautiful creations, or whether he should boldly mark out a track for himself, and in leading a new people to national independence, trample down all opposition. During most of the day he rode along in silence, and none of his companions disturbed his reveries. Towards evening he addressed them—he made a rapid but clear survey of events that had passed—contemplated the present state of affairs, and dwelt upon the future prospects of Texas with enthusiasm. He seemed to read her future as the ancient prophets did the history of Judah. He had fixed his purpose, and all the world could not move him. After making an official report to the governor, he proceeded with his Aide-de-Camp, Major Hockley, to the Cherokee Nation, in pursuance of instructions received from the Consultation, to form treaties with that and other Indian tribes. He met the Indians in Council, and having been returned as a delegate to the Convention which was to meet in Washington on the 1st of March, he arrived there the day previous. The Convention assembled and organized, and the following day, the 2d, of March, 1836, the DECLARATION OF INDEPENDENCE was adopted and signed.

CHAPTER VII:
THE GENERAL

The Declaration of Independence, for which public feeling had been precipitately matured, was adopted unanimously, and hailed throughout Texas with joy and acclamation. So was it received, too, by the people of the United States, wherever they had even a faint conception of the issue made in the struggle, or the vast magnitude of the consequences that were to follow.

But from the hour the news that Texas had declared herself free and independent reached the United States, a feeling of hostility was excited against the infant Republic, without a parallel in the history of the world. Losing sight of the grand moral results that were to flow from that event, and unmindful even of the hour of our own heroism, when we extended our feeble hands to France for help, a chorus burst of indignation went up from a thousand newspapers, and everywhere the Declaration of Texian Independence was declared to be an act of high-banded robbery, perpetrated by a band of bold outlaws. To have emigrated to that part of the world was enough to brand a man with infamy; and those who gave the little they could afford to help on the struggle, cast their mite into the Texian Treasury in silence. All recollection of our fathers and the days of their dark struggles seemed to be as completely obliterated from the memory of many of our countrymen, as though they had been swept by the waters of oblivion. We forgot that the men, who were fighting those battles, were many of them descended from the early settlers of Jamestown and Plymouth; that hearts were nerved there for the defense of liberty, whose fathers had poured out their blood at Yorktown and Saratoga, and Bennington, and Bunker Hill! And who were the men that joined in this ten years' crusade against the liberties of a Sister Republic? And how would the victors of San Jacinto have been laughed away by them in scorn from our altars of confederate freedom, if they had not themselves been crushed by the simultaneous rising of an indignant people at the last election!

Some days before the Declaration was adopted, letters had been received from Travis, in command of the Alamo at Bexar, notifying the *people* of Texas, for there were then no chief authorities of the country, that he was invested by a numerous force in the Alamo, calling loudly for help. Houston, it will be remembered, anticipating this very result, had given orders to the commanding officer to abandon and blow up the Alamo; but his orders had been disobeyed by the officer, and treated with contempt by the General Council, who had ordered the commander to defend the place to the last, promising to reinforce him. And now the brave men in the Alamo were to atone for the treachery and low ambition of a few selfish men. The promised reinforcement was limited to *thirty men*, making Travis' whole effective force not more than one hundred and eighty-five, and they without a month's provisions, detached from all Texian settlements more than seventy miles, and the intervening territory swept by the Mexican cavalry.

As the provisional government, by which Houston had been elected commander-in-chief, had ceased when the Convention assembled, he resigned his Major-Generalship. But there was no other man in Texas to whom the people could look in this emergency. The Convention went into the election of a commander-in-chief, and out of fifty-six votes, Houston, who was not present, received all but one vote. Texas had no organization of forces, and the few gallant men from Georgia and Alabama in the field were detached beyond the southern settlements, under the command of a man who had treated the orders of the commander-in-chief with contempt. The treatment Houston had received from the Council was known, and the people feared he would decline the office. A deep gloom now hung over the public mind. Apprehension and alarm were written on every face, and the conviction became almost universal that the cause of Texian independence was lost unless Houston would accept the command of the army. Impressed with the general feeling, and stirred by the heroic spirit which has always guided him, he resolved to peril everything, and stake life itself upon the issue, and he accepted the command.

On Sunday, the 6th of March, a letter was received from Col. Travis, addressed to the President of the Convention, brought by the last express that ever left the Alamo. The intelligence it conveyed was no sooner known, than an electric terror flashed through the community. The members, and a crowd of spectators, rushed to the hall of the convention, the president to his chair, the members to their seats, without summons or signal. The president rose, and announced the receipt of a document of the most important character ever received by any assembly of men. He then read a letter from Col. Travis, of the most thrilling character. It was written in all the fervor of patriotic and devoted courage; but it breathed the language of despair. Robert Potter rose, and moved that "the Convention do immediately adjourn, arm, and march to the relief of the Alamo." Houston, feeling that the next movement made in the Convention would be likely to decide the fate of Texas, determined what should be done by the Convention as well as by himself.

All eyes were turned upon him, and as he rose from his seat, it would seem that, for a moment, every heart in the assembly stopped beating. He opposed the motion, and denounced it as madness, worse than treason, to the people. They had, to be sure, declared themselves independent but they had yet no organization. There must be a government, and it must have organic form—without it, they would be nothing but outlaws, and could hope neither for the sympathy nor respect of mankind. He spoke nearly an hour, and his appeal, if he ever was eloquent, was eloquence itself. He admonished the Convention of the peril of the country; he advised them to sit calmly, and firmly and coolly pursue their deliberations; to be wise and patriotic; to feel no alarm, and he pledged himself instantly to repair to Gonzales, where he had heard that a small corps of militia had rallied, and interpose them between the Convention and the enemy; and while they chose to sit in Convention, the Mexicans should never approach them unless they marched over his dead body. In the meantime, if mortal power could avail, he would relieve the brave men in the Alamo.

Houston stopped speaking, and walked immediately out of the Convention. In less than an hour he was mounted on his battle horse, and with three or four brave companions was on his way to the Alamo. Men looked upon it as an idle and desperate attempt, or surely more would have followed him. The party rode hard that day, and only stopped late at night to rest their horses. They were now in the open prairie. At break of day, Houston retired some distance from the party, and listened intensely, as if expecting a distant signal. Col. Travis had stated in his letters, that as long as the Alamo could hold out against the invaders, signal guns would be fired at sunrise. It is a well authenticated fact, that for many successive days, these guns had been heard at a distance of nearly two hundred miles across the prairie—and being now within the reach of their sound, Houston was anxiously waiting for the expected signal. The day before, like many preceding it, a dull, rumbling murmur had come booming over the prairie like distant thunder. He listened with an acuteness of sense which no man can understand but one whose bearing has been sharpened by the teachings of the dwellers of the forest, and who is awaiting a signal of life or death from brave men. He listened in vain. Not the faintest murmur came floating on the calm, morning air. He knew the Alamo had fallen, and he returned to tell his companions. The event confirmed his convictions, for the Alamo had fired its last gun the morning he left Washington; and at the very moment he was speaking in the Convention, those brave men were meeting their fate.

After returning to his companions, who were preparing to pursue their march, he wrote a letter to the Convention recommending them to adopt a resolution *declaring Texas a part of Louisiana under the Treaty of 1803*. His suggestion was not adopted, but if he had been there to enforce it by his commanding eloquence, it would doubtless have been passed—for in those deliberative assemblies he was as absolute as ever Cromwell was in the Rump Parliament, with a thousand bayonets at his back. In this case, too, he would have had the means of conviction in the policy he proposed. Such a measure would have won for them the sympathies of legislatures as well as peoples. They would not then have been regarded as a separate people. It would have matured the Republic and its institutions; it would have shortened the period of her struggles. Neither the question of recognition nor annexation would have been raised—she would have been *adopted* at once. Houston looked at the whole matter with the eye of a statesman and the heart of a soldier. He knew that Mexico would have withdrawn at once from the conflict, if Texas had *at once* been constituted a part of Louisiana.

If, then, it be asked, why Mexico has, at last, not only made war upon Texas, after the Great Powers recognized her independence, but against the United States after annexation we answer, that there is no man who knows enough about this subject to qualify him to hazard an opinion who does not understand and believe that Mexico has been emboldened to provoke the war, only because of the long, powerful, persevering, and desperate hostility with which a thousand newspapers and a thousand public men, in this country, have resisted the annexation. These presses and these public men have held the very same language, and displayed the very same spirit towards Texas, that Santa Anna, and Bravo, and Bustamente, and Almonte, and Herrera, and Paredes, and their hireling presses, have done. In fact, the hopes of these military despots have all rested upon the efforts of the enemies of Texas in the United

States, and not upon their popularity at home, or the power of their cannon, or the justice of their cause. In New York, and Philadelphia, and Boston, they have stationed their most trustworthy and confidential agents; here they have expended their money, and here their battles have been fought. Who of those bold, impudent tyrants would have dared to tread upon a single fold of the mantle that wrapped the youthful form of Texian Liberty, if its very name had not been made a by-word among the children of the heroes of '76. It is known that Paredes never apprehended any danger of being brought to battle; he never expected he would be called on to make good his braggart threats. And now when this mad hostility against Texas has been frowned down by the American people, and its grand movers are glad enough of the first chance that is offered to redeem their American character, they throw off the Mexican disguise and vote the ten millions and the fifty thousand volunteers with loud huzzas, throw up their cap to the heroes of Palo Alto and La Resaca de la Palma, and wish to make the hero of this "accursed war" President of the United States. And of all the boasters and bullies who damned Mr. Polk for sending the heroic Taylor to the Rio Grande, not one of them all has dared to open his mouth against the war after the first victory, except the editor of the New York Tribune, who, with all his non-resistance principles and all his other *isms*, has shown that he possesses more genuine courage than the whole phalanx together. "Oh! shame, where is thy blush"—and echo answers where?

The Alamo had fired its last gun, and its brave defenders had met their fate. But Houston proceeded to Gonzales, although not a man joined him on the road. On setting out from the Convention, he dispatched an express to Fannin, directing him to form a junction with him on the Cibolo, a small river between Gonzales and San Antonio, intending with the united forces to march to the relief of the Alamo. About the 10th of March (1836) he reached Gonzales, where he found

874 men. They were without organization, and destitute of supplies—they were neither armed nor clad for the campaign. He at once had them assembled and organized, the men electing their own officers. Scouts who had been dispatched to the neighborhood of San Antonio, returned about the time of Houston's arrival, under the impression that the Alamo had fallen. This created some sensation among the troops, and immediately afterwards two Mexicans, whose families had resided among the American colonists, came in from the region of San Antonio and confirmed the general apprehension. Houston, who was satisfied that their statement was correct, had it written down. It represented that the Alamo had been taken on the morning of the 6th of March, and every human being in it slaughtered, except a woman, her child, and a negro: that after their slaughter, the dead had been dragged out and piled together with wood in one vast hecatomb, and burned to ashes.

When the news of this act of cold-blooded barbarity flew through the colonies, it stirred up a spirit that would never sleep again. But the day of vengeance was rapidly coming— the hour of San Jacinto was not far off. Houston immediately sent another express to Fannin (March 11th), apprising him of the fall of the Alamo, and ordering him to evacuate Goliad, blow up the fortress, and fall back without delay upon Victoria and the Gaudelupe. This would unite all the forces then in the field, which Houston regarded as the only means of saving Texas. Fannin's force, the general estimated at over 500, and once joined to his own, the army would number at least 900 effective men, since Fannin had a fine supply of arms brought from the United States.

This order reached Fannin some eight days before he attempted a retreat; indeed he did not attempt it at all, till he had been surrounded by the Mexicans several days. In reply to the orders of the commander-in-chief, Fannin sent an express, saying he had held a council of war, and had concluded to defend the place, and had named it Fort Defiance. He also said, he was prepared to abide the consequences of disobeying his orders. The sequel showed but too well how prophetic was the glance Houston cast over the future.

On the twelfth (we believe) of March, about 8 o'clock in the evening, Mrs. Dickinson arrived with her child at Gen. Houston's camp, accompanied by two negro guides, sent to attend her by Santa Anna, and also to bring a proclamation of pardon to the insurgent colonists, if they would lay down their arms. The proclamation was, of course, treated as such papers had been by our fathers, when they were sent to their camps of suffering by the myrmidon general of a British king. Mrs. Dickinson was the wife of one of the brave officers whose bones had crumbled on the sacrificial pyre of the Alamo. Houston was walking alone, a few hundred yards from the camp, at the moment this stricken and bereaved messenger arrived. He returned soon after, and found that her fearful narrative of the butchering and burning, with some of the most stirring details of that dark tragedy, had already struck the soldiers with a chill of horror; and when she told them that 5,000 men were advancing by forced marches, and their artillery would soon be heard at Gonzales, the wildest consternation spread through the camp. Their alarm soon reached a pitch of desperation. Some were stunned with silence, others were wild with lamentations, and even officers had set fire to their tents.

When Houston came up; he ordered silence, and the fires to be extinguished. He then addressed the soldiery in the most fervid manner, and they all gathered around him, except a few who had at the first impulse fled for their horses. He detached a guard instantly to intercept fugitives, and more than twenty were brought back sneaking to the camp. But a few good runners made their escape to the settlements and carried panic in every direction!

The general announced to his comrades that he should that night fall back to a more secure position, as they were in a bend of the river, where the enemy, by crossing, could cut off all possible retreat. Accordingly, about eleven o'clock that night, Houston ordered every light in Gonzales to be extinguished, and leaving a rear-guard with orders to use the utmost vigilance and give information of the first approach of the enemy, he ordered the camp to be struck, and the little band took up their line of march in good order. On reaching Gonzales, feeling assured that the disasters which finally followed, were inevitable, he had ordered all the women and children to be transported to the interior settlements, for throughout the entire Texian struggle, he was resolved that the helpless should never be left to the tender mercies of the Mexicans. Before the crisis came, he hoped the transports would return, but in this he was disappointed, and that night the entire army was followed by only one baggage wagon, which was drawn by four oxen.

He continued his march that night to Peach Creek, ten, miles from Gonzales, and halted to refresh the troops. He was here met by a reinforcement of a hundred men, which increased his army to upwards of four hundred and fifty. The fugitives from Gonzales had met this company and given them the news from the Alamo, and so anxious had they become, that nearly one quarter of them had left their officers to hurry on to the camp. About daybreak, an hour after the arrival of the army at the Creek, an explosion was heard in the direction of Gonzales. It produced an electrical effect upon the army, and many exclaimed it was the enemy's cannon. Another and a third explosion were heard in quick succession. Houston afterwards said that they were the most agreeable sounds he had ever heard. On the march that night, he was informed that several barrels of intoxicating liquors, left in a store at Gonzales, had been poisoned by arsenic, and he denounced it as a monstrous act, and not to be justified even by the barbarities of their savage foe. Understanding at once the cause of the explosions, Houston quieted their apprehensions by announcing the cause. It has been stated that Houston had ordered the town of Gonzales to be reduced to ashes; but credible men who were there, declared that the charge was not only false, but that he was angry when he heard the fact. The gallant Captain Karnes, who had been left in command of the rear-guard, believing its destruction would be an annoyance to the enemy, and deprive them of the merchandise and other supplies, had set the town on fire. After a halt of three hours, the army continued their march to the Brazos. At the Lavaca he received the letter from Colonel Fannin, which has already been referred to, and he is said to have turned to his aide-de-camp, Major Hockley, and pointing to the little band which seemed but a speck on the vast prairie, said, "Hockley, there is the last hope of Texas. We shall never see Fannin nor his men—with these soldiers we must achieve our independence or perish in the attempt." It was a sad and gloomy march. Over the fatal tragedy of the Alamo seemed to come the dirge of 500 more devoted men.

Towards evening, they perceived, at a distance, a small moving mass in the advance, which soon proved to be a company of some thirty volunteers, from the Brazos, under Captain Splann. Even this diffused some cheerfulness, and added to the lustre of the setting sun an additional ray.

At night they encamped on the Lavaca, where Houston created a volunteer aide-de-camp of Major Wm. T. Austin, and dispatched him to the settlements of the Brazos, to meet him with supplies of cannon, &c., on the Colorado, where he intended to make a stand against the enemy. A person present has given a graphic account of a scene that occurred that night in a little shanty. Hockley was sitting by a rude table, writing down orders for Austin, which were dictated by his general, who was feeding a little fire with oak splinters, to furnish them the only light their extremities allowed them.

On the assurance of Austin that supplies could be obtained, Houston had directed him to bring not less than seven pieces of mounted cannon, with mules sufficient for draught, and at least twelve good horses for his spies, with ammunition sufficient for the artillery. The march was continued to the Navi-dad—where intelligence reached him that a blind woman and her seven children had been passed by, and were not apprised that the enemy was approaching. The general immediately detached a company of fifty men, under two confidential officers, and delayed his march till the woman and her little orphans were brought safely to the camp.

We have before us a dispatch written by Houston, "from the camp on the Navidad," to the chairman of the Military Committee, dated March 15, from which we make a few extracts:

> My morning report, on my arrival at the camp, showed 374 men, without two days' provisions; many without arms, and others without ammunition. We could have met the enemy and avenged some of our wrongs; but, as we were, without supplies for men in the camp, either of provisions, ammunition, or artillery, and remote from succor, it would have been madness to have hazarded a contest.
>
> * * The first principles of the drill had not been taught the men.* * If the camp had once been broken up there would have been no hope for the future. * * *I am fearful Goliad is besieged by the enemy. All orders to Col. Fannin, directing the place to be blown up, and the cannon to be sunk in the river, and to fall back on Victoria, would reach him before the enemy could advance.* * I directed, on the 16th of January last, that the artillery should be moved and the* ALAMO *blown up; but it was prevented by the expedition upon Matamoros, the cause of all our misfortunes."*

These extracts show, beyond a question, that the horrid slaughter at the Alamo was foreseen by Houston, and caused by *violating his orders.* Also, that the still more bloody tragedy of Goliad was in the commander's eye before it happened, and caused in like manner by disobeying his orders. The lives of hundreds of the bravest men paid the penalty, and Texas did not recover from the fatal consequences for many years.

From the Navidad he marched on to the Colorado, where he halted till all the women and children, and non-combatants, with their cattle and horses, had safely crossed over. Leaving a guard on his rear, he went over the Colorado with the main army. On this day, 17th of March, he thus writes the Military

Committee:

> Today, at half-past four p.m., we reached this Point (Burnham's). *
> * It pains me at heart that such consternation should be spread by
> a few deserters from the camp, but we are here, and if only three
> hundred men remain on this side the Brazos, I will die with them or
> conquer our enemies. * * Send agents to the United States. Appeal
> to them in the holy names of Liberty and Humanity. * * Let the men
> from the East of the Trinity rush to us. Let all the disposable force
> of Texas fly to arms."

On the following day he marched down the eastern bank of
the Colorado, about twelve miles, and encamped opposite Beason's, to await the arrival of Austin with his supplies. During
this period he had to keep pickets for more than thirty miles
up and down the river, to prevent surprise. Shortly after his arrival, it was ascertained that General Sezma had advanced to
the opposite side of the river, and taken a position a few miles
above the Texian camp, which caused Houston's rear-guard
to fall back over the river. They had, without authority from
their general, set fire to Burnham's premises, as the enemy had
encamped nearby.

Houston now sent a detachment with orders to secret themselves in a strong position, supposing that the army would be
likely to pass the river with a strong advance guard, and the
position of the Texians being well chosen, would enable them
to discomfit five times their number. As he had anticipated, the
enemy crossed the river with upwards of 50 cavalry, unconscious of the ambuscade, and would have been completely cut
off, had it not been for the imprudence of one man, who fired
upon them too soon, and thus advertised them of their danger.
No other attempt was made to cross.

Some few reinforcements and supplies reached the camp
about this time. But his entire force, including all his detach-
ments, did not exceed 650 men; and his artillery not arriving,
he was unable to cross the river and give battle to General
Sezma. Austin had limited his arrival with the supplies and ar-

tillery to twelve days, and although the time had passed, nothing had yet been heard from him. A slight skirmish had taken place between a party of riflemen and an advance guard of the enemy, but without any decisive result. On the 23d March, Houston writes to Mr. Rusk:

> You know I am not easily depressed, but, before my God, since we parted, I have found the darkest hours of my life. For forty-eight hours I have neither eaten an ounce of anything, nor have I slept. All who saw the deserters, breathed the poison and fled. It was a poor compliment to me to suppose I would not advise the Convention of any necessity that might have arisen for the removal.

In the midst of all this gloom and suspense, the news came, which burst like a bolt of thunder over the little army—*Colonel Fannin's Regiment had all been massacred!* A Mexican, by the name of Peter Kerr, had brought the intelligence, and although he had not a shadow of doubt the man's story was true, yet such was the alarm it had created, the general was obliged to throw discredit upon the messenger, to prevent his camp from being deserted. The fall of the Alamo had well nigh dispersed the little army, and when they heard that 500 brave comrades, fully armed and equipped, had all been cut off, their consternation was redoubled. The last barrier between them and a slaughtering army seemed swept away, and it was not strange that this last sad news had unnerved their courage.

Houston had his part to play that night, and he played it well. In such exigencies all the difficulties have to be overcome *at once.* He instantly called for the sergeant of the guard, and denouncing Kerr as an incendiary of the Mexicans, sent to his camp to produce distraction, declared in a furious passion he would have the spy shot the next morning at nine o'clock. An order was immediately given to have the man arrested and placed under a strong guard. He then addressed the soldiery, and adduced many reasons why the news could not be true. His apparent disbelief calmed the excitement, which had reached a fearful pitch. Houston would not see the prisoner till the camp had retired to rest. He then went to the guard-fire, and heard his story. He knew that his worst apprehensions had become history. He gave private orders to have his prisoner treated kindly, and the next morning he forgot to have him executed! The excitement had passed away with the dreams of the soldiers—but the prisoner could not be released at once, since everything which savored of the Mexicans was odious to the army, and Houston would have been charged with turning loose a spy, and perhaps collusion with the enemy. Houston struck his camp that evening, and marched towards the Brazos. The army reached San Felipe the next night, effecting a march of about twenty-eight miles in less than twenty-four hours. We find in one of the general's dispatches, dated

CAMP, WEST OF THE BRAZOS, MARCH 31ST.

My intention was to have attacked the enemy on the second night after the day Fannin's destruction was reported by Kerr. * * Send me daily expresses, and let me know what to rely on. I must let the camp know something, and I want everything promised, to be realized by them, and I can keep them together. I have thus far succeeded beyond my hopes. I will do the best I can; but be assured, the fame of Jackson could never compensate me for my anxiety and mental pain. Two nights since, when it was reported that the enemy was on this side of the Colorado, the citizens of San Felipe reduced it to ashes. There was no order from me for it.

On the 3d of April, Houston again writes the Secretary of War. After describing the massacre of Fannin's command, he says:

Humanity must recoil at the perfidy which has been exercised towards brave and heroic men, who have perished in the unequal conflicts with the enemy, when they were always more than six to one. Will not our friends rush to the conflict, and at once avenge the wrongs which have been indicted on our dauntless comrades? The day of just retribution ought not to be deferred.

Again, on the 6th of April, he says:

The enemy shall be closely looked to, and the first favorable moment seized with avidity, to effect his total defeat.

The army encamped on the night of the 29th of March at Mill Creek, and the following day reached their destination opposite Groce's. The steamboat *Yellow Stone*, which was lying at the landing, was at once pressed into the service, and a company of troops stationed on board to prevent the boat or its engineers from running off. The army remained in the same position till the 11th of April. During this time the river had swollen by the spring rains, and as Houston's camp lay on an island of the Brazos, where he was secure from the enemy, he constructed a narrow bridge, by which communication was maintained with the enemy's country, over which the Texian scouts could pass, to gather information, and hold a keen vigilance of the movements and designs of the Mexicans.

Before the waters reached their greatest height, General Houston had designed, as soon as the enemy should approach San Felipe, to march with all his force and surprise them at night, believing that their confidence, inspired by numbers, discipline, and success, would have completely thrown them off their guard, which would give an easy victory to the Texian commander. But when he learned of the arrival of the enemy at San Felipe, the freshet was at its height, and having three creeks without fords to pass in his march, this boldly conceived plan failed. Although no fortunate result followed many of these designs of Houston, yet they will show to the reader the sleepless vigilance and bold daring of the man upon whose movements was suspended the fate of the young Commonwealth. We also deem their relation important, because they serve to render the reader familiar with the chances and changes of warfare, and the qualities necessary in the citizen who leads an army to the field.

The company left in charge of San Felipe having retired to the east side of the river, and thrown up a partial fortification of timber, the enemy immediately opened their artillery upon their breastworks, and the noise of their cannon announced to Houston the first *certainty* of their approach. A company of eighty men, which had just arrived at the camp from Eastern Texas, were detached with another body to succor Captain Baker, while, by means of expresses, the Commander-in-Chief kept up communication with the troops at San Felipe and Fort Bend.

His entire force at Groce's, where the main body of the army lay, did not now exceed five hundred and twenty men. He had been encouraged to expect not less than five hundred men from the Redlands, and they could have been furnished, for they were already in the field, and many of them had advanced their march to the banks of the Trinity. But some turbulent men, who were willing to ruin the country rather than fail in Houston's destruction, raised rumors of Indian hostilities, which prevented them from joining him. Amongst them was General Quitman's command from Natchez—a fine company of southern chivalry, who were thus prevented from participating in the triumphs of San Jacinto. They arrived at the camp two days after the victory. The country behind Houston was entirely depopulated. He never fell back till the women and children were secure from danger—always interposing the army between the enemy and the helpless.

He had now become apprised of the strength, position and designs of the enemy. They were marching upon him in three divisions. The center was to advance from San Antonio to Gonzales, Beason's, and by San Felipe or Washington, and Robbins' Ferry to Nacogdoches—led by Santa Anna himself. The Second Division, under General Urrea, was to march from Goliad by the way of Victoria to Brazoria and Harrisburg, while the upper or Third Division advanced by Bastrop to Tenoxtitlan on the Brazos, and thence to the Comanche crossing the Trinity, on to Nacogdoches. The plan of the campaign gave evidence of the superior ability of Santa Anna, and showed Houston the man he had to deal with. At the same time the entire scheme had to be broken up in less than thirty days, or Texas would be swept by three rolling streams of fire, which would cover the land with desolation, and blot out the last hope of the Republic. How this almost impossible work was to be achieved, no one knew but Houston. There was a painful feeling of suspense throughout the little army, and all eyes were turned anxiously upon their bold leader. There was no longer a doubt in the mind of anyone who knew the position of affairs, that the salvation of Texas, under God, had been thrown entirely upon Houston's arm.

What was his policy? Apprised of all this, he believed that the divisions were sufficiently detached to be managed in detail, if the succors he had a right to expect should reach him in time. His position on the Brazos enabled him to cover a larger extent of country than any other he could have selected, and was one of the most eligible for supplies. During his entire encampment there he was sending frequent expresses to Eastern Texas, and while he represented his true situation in his confidential dispatches to the Committee of Vigilance and Safety at Nacogdoches, he was in the habit, we have heard, of endorsing the envelopes with certain postscripts, that all might see that his force did not exceed twenty-five hundred men; for he believed if his real situation was known, it would deter all succors from coming to his aid. This is the only origin we have discovered for the report of his having so large a command.

About the 11th of April, news came from Fort Bend that the Center Division under Santa Anna had already crossed the river at that place. The company stationed there not maintaining the vigilance enjoined, the ferry-boat was taken over by a negro to the western side. By this means they were enabled ,at once to pass the river. Had it not been for this circumstance, the Brazos being at high flood, they could not have passed for a month, and Houston could have maintained his position till his safety inspired a confidence that would have reinforced his army.

A fortunate combination of circumstances enabled Houston to maintain himself against the influence that seemed to be marking his destiny. The Upper Division of the Mexican army, under Gaono, became bewildered in their march, and ascended the Colorado. The South Division under Urrea, was delayed by high waters, and never passed the Brazos at all. Santa Anna had, doubtless, learned that Harrisburg had become the seat of government, after the adjournment of the Convention, which took place on the 17th of March, and was prepared to take advantage of the alarm which this flight of the officers of the Republic had spread over the colonies. The Convention had broken up in utter consternation and dismay, and only seven of its members ever found their way to the army. None but those who were on the ground can have any conception of the fatal consequences that attended this movement. It is safe, probably, to say that to it more than any other cause was it owing that Houston received no more reinforcements in that trying crisis. A constitutional act had been passed by the Convention, creating a government *ad interim*, consisting of a president, and secretaries of war, navy, and the treasury, with all powers incident to a government, except the lawmaking. They had adjourned to Harrisburg, not less than seventy miles from the scene of war. The wise men and the worthies of the nation, thus fleeing from danger, was calculated to alarm the old, the young, and the helpless, to afford an excuse to the timid, and sanction the flight of the cowardly. Many brave men who had joined Houston, hearing of the general consternation which had followed the adjournment of the Convention, could not resist their natural impulses to go and render protection to their abandoned fugitive wives and children. Houston has often declared that this was one of the most appalling circumstances that ever befell him while struggling for Texas, and we find this confirmed by his dispatches.

But the event proved it was fortunate for him that Santa Anna had heard that Harrisburg had become the seat of government, for it caused him to abandon his general plan of invasion, and diverge from his route to Nacogdoches, with a view to capture the self-preserving administration of the new Republic. As soon as General Houston received intelligence that Santa Anna was crossing the Brazos, he dispatched without delay his orders for all the troops, scattered up and down the river, from Washington to Fort Bend, a distance of more than eighty miles, to join him on his march to Harrisburg. While he lay on the Brazos, General Rusk, now Senator from Texas, and then newly-appointed Secretary of War, instead of flying from the scene of danger, when the rest of the cabinet fled, hastened to the commander-in-chief on the Brazos. They advised together most cordially, on all matters connected with the welfare of Texas, and harmonized most perfectly in the means necessary to be adopted.

The steamboat *Yellow Stone* was put in motion, and in two days the entire army, with their baggage-wagons and horses, was transported to the eastern side of the Brazos. On the shore, Houston met the first artillery which had been under his control. They were two six-pounders (a present from some patriotic men in Cincinnati), but they were without equipments necessary for use, except that they were mounted. There being a smith's shop and gunsmiths there, who had been employed in repairing the arms of the troops, the two field-pieces were immediately made ready for effective use, and all the old iron in the neighborhood cut into slugs, and formed into cartridges. The little army halted a few miles from the ferry, and encamped for the night. After the commander-in-chief had, as was his uniform custom, examined in person the state of the camp, and seen that everything necessary for an early march had been done, he inquired the route for Harrisburg. Houston had never before been in that region, but he took the precaution to inform himself perfectly of the geography of the country, well knowing that he was liable to be surprised any hour by a superior force. One road led to Nacogdoches, crossing the Trinity at Robbins' Ferry; and Houston knew that this was the road Santa Anna must have taken in his march upon Harrisburg. The main army, amounting to between seven and eight hundred men, was now put in motion. They marched that day (16th April) to McArley's, a fatiguing march of eighteen miles, through a prairie. There were fourteen baggage wagons, and two pieces of artillery in the train. Excessive rains had made the prairie boggy, and in many places the wagons had to be unloaded, and the dismounted field-pieces carried or rolled through the mire. This brought into requisition the entire physical strength of the army. Houston had, early in the march, foreseen what lay before his men, and on the first emergency, he stripped off his coat, dismounted, and set the example of unloading and transporting baggage and guns, and so continued throughout the day, commanding and aiding the soldiers with his personal strength. The brave little army halted at sunset, and laid themselves down to sleep in the open field, without covering, for there was not a tent in the camp. About dark, a cold rain set in, and continued for twenty-four hours. Such were the hardships those men were compelled to undergo, who were working out the emancipation of their country.

The second day (17th) they pursued their exhausting march through the rain, twelve miles, to Burnett's settlement, which they found deserted. Another night followed—the soldiers slept on the wet ground, with their arms in their hands, ready to answer in a single moment the three taps of the drum, which was the only instrument of martial music in the camp, and which was never touched but by the general himself. The third day's march (18th), through the prairie, of eighteen miles, brought them to Post Oak Bayou, where they encamped for the night. Their toilsome march through the prairie was now over, and they were only six or eight miles from Harrisburg. But Santa Anna had been there before them, and reduced the town to ashes, on his march to New Washington.

The army had marched up within two miles of the stream, and almost in sight of the ruin, and prepared to cross the Buf-

falo Bayou, which lay between them and the scene of desolation. The gallant Karnes, and Deaf Smith, swam over the
stream with several companions, and in a short time brought
back over the bayou two expresses who bore most important
intelligence. On the person of the courier, who was a Mexican officer, were found dispatches from Filisola to Santa Anna,
so recently written, that the reader remarked: "The ink, sir, is
hardly dry." The Texian commander now had the most positive assurance that Santa Anna was in command of the advance of the enemy. The second express contained the mail
from the capital, filled with letters of congratulation recognizing Santa Anna as Emperor of Mexico, &c.

Mr. Rusk, the Secretary of War, and General Houston, immediately retired for a private conference. Very few words
passed between them: the facts were before them, and they
could come to but one decision. "We need not talk," said the
general, "you think we ought to fight, and I think so too." The
battle was decided on, and the fate of Texas was to be settled
as soon as the enemy could be found. Shortly after this conference, General Houston was informed by Colonel Hockley that
he had overheard an officer in command of a regiment saying to the men about him, over whom he supposed himself to
possess the greatest influence, "Boys, Houston don't intend to
fight—follow me and you shall have enough of it." Houston at
once remarked to Hockley, "I'll cure this mischief directly." He
ordered the two colonels to be sent for. "Gentlemen, have you
rations of beef in the camp, for three days?" "Yes, sir." "You
will then see that each man is supplied with three days' cooked
rations, and hold the camp in readiness to march. We will see
if we can find Santa Anna. Good morning, gentlemen." Turning off with Hockley, Houston remarked, "There is no excuse
for sedition now, if they wish to fight." At the same time orders
were given to prepare for crossing the bayou—that the army
might commence their march the next morning upon the enemy.

Night passed, and daylight came—but no preparations had been made for the march. The orders of the commanding officer had been disregarded, and not a soldier was prepared with his rations. Not a moment was to be lost. Instead of taking his rest, as was his custom early in the morning, the general issued his orders himself to the men, and the camp was soon busy with the note of preparation. But it was nine o'clock before he could get his column under arms. When the army arrived at the bayou, two miles from the encampment, they found the boat nearly filled with water. Houston at once dismounted, called for an axe, and went to hewing oars out of rails.

The passage was a difficult and perilous undertaking, and yet Houston was determined to make it that morning. The bayou was about fifty yards wide, and more than twenty feet deep. As the Pioneers, a small company, were going aboard, an accident occurred which damaged the boat. Houston leaped aboard at once; and his faithful horse, whom he had left pawing on the bank, plunged in after his master, and swam to the opposite shore. A rope was soon constructed out of cabriestas (a rope of horse hair) and raw tugs, and fastened to both sides of the stream, which enabled the boat to make more rapid trips, and kept it from floating downstream. The passage was now being made with great rapidity, but it was an hour of intense anxiety to the commander and his intelligent councilor, the Secretary of War. General Houston had crossed, and stood on one side, while Mr. Rusk remained on the other, both watching the perilous movement of their little army, in whose brave hearts the hopes of Texas were now all gathered. A single accident! No one knew but the next moment the enemy's column might heave in sight, and if they came up while that deep stream divided the army of Texas, the result would be foretold before it happened.

Half the army had now passed, and of course it was the moment of the deepest peril. The boat was giving way; four strong men were bailing out the water continually. The body of cavalry was now to be risked. They were goaded to plunge into the deep stream, and they at once disappeared. But they rose again in their strength and strained for the steep bank. They reached it, and when they struck the solid ground they sprang from the water, and shook their tired limbs. The passage was made. Mr. Rusk went over on the last boat. It was an affecting spectacle to see these two brave men seize each other's hands when they met on the left bank of the stream; and it is not difficult to believe what is indeed said, that the same expression of gratitude fell from their lips together—"Thank God—we are at last safely over." While the lines were forming, General Houston drew from his pocket a scrap of paper, and with a pencil (here was his only portfolio) wrote the following letter.

Camp at Harrisburg, April 19th, 1836.
To Colonel Rusk in the Field,

This morning we are in preparation to meet Santa, Anna. It is the only chance of saving Texas. From time to time I have looked for reinforcements in vain. The Convention's adjourning to Harrisburg struck panic throughout the country. Texas could have started at least four thousand men. We will only be about seven hundred to march, besides the camp guard. But we go to conquest. It is wisdom growing out of necessity to meet and fight the enemy now. Every consideration enforces it. The troops are in fine spirits, and now is the time for action. We will use our best efforts to fight the enemy to such advantage as will insure victory, though the odds are greatly against us. I leave the result in the hands of an all-wise God, and I rely confidently upon His providence. My country will do justice to those who serve her. The right for which we fight will be secured, and Texas shall be free.

SAMUEL HOUSTON, Commander-in-Chief.
(Certified copy from the Department of War, of the Republic of Texas.)

The lines were now formed, and Houston rode up and addressed the soldiers. Those who heard him, say that he made the most impassioned and eloquent appeal they ever listened to. The words seemed to flow along the lines like streams of electric fluid, and when he gave them for their watchword, Re-

MEMBER THE ALAMO, it struck like a bolt of fire. The watchword had no sooner fallen from his lips, than it was caught up by every man in the army, and one simultaneous shout broke up into the sky—*Remember the Alamo, Remember the Alamo*, was repeated, and the green islands of trees in the prairie sent back the echo. The Secretary of War also spoke in the most happy and stirring manner. The men seemed inspired with the spirit of chivalry, and were impatient for the order of "March" to be given.

The order came, and the column got under way. As it moved on over the prairie, the golden sun shone out full and clear from mid-heaven, as it never shines even in that beautiful climate, except after a long cold rain. It seemed to be the signal of God's approval, and they felt that the Heavens themselves smiled on the struggle. No martial strains fell upon the ear, no rich bugle rang out its full clear blast, no gorgeous banners waved over the embattled host. Their march was not measured even by "the thrilling fife, the pealing drum." There was little of the pomp or circumstance of glorious war, but there was the firm purpose, the strained muscle, the compressed lip, and the heavy tramp of seven hundred men, determined to be free.

In a narrow woodland not far from the stream, the army halted till sundown, to avoid being seen in the open prairie. The column was now once more in motion, and a forced march made to a point not more than four or five miles distant from the ground where the main struggle was to be made. They took shelter under the cover of a grove off from the line of march, and the weary men laid down on their rifles to sleep for an hour.

At daylight General Houston rose from the ground where he had been resting his head on a coil of rope used in dragging the artillery, and roused the camp by his well known three taps of the drum—for a reveille or tattoo had never been beaten from the day he took the command. Their artillery had never been fired till it was fired in the face of the enemy.

Pickets were advanced in every direction. The scouts sent on ahead soon returned with information which satisfied the commander the enemy was not far distant. A small party had been fallen in with, and chase given to them, but they were well mounted, and effected their escape. On the return of the scouting party, the army halted to take refreshment, beeves were dressed, and the roasting-fires kindled.

But little progress had been made when, about seven o'clock that same morning, news came that the enemy was marching up from New Washington to cross the San Jacinto, which, if effected, would have enabled Santa Anna to carry desolation to the Sabine. Houston immediately ordered the line to be taken up for the crossing of the San Jacinto at Lynchburg. The issue of the entire struggle hinged on cutting off Santa Anna's retreat. The army saw it at once. The soldiers, with alacrity, abandoned their meat half-cooked, flew to their arms as one man, and as soon as the horses could be hitched to the artillery the march began. The column did not halt till the ferry at the junction of Buffalo Bayou and the San Jacinto was reached, where, to the great joy of the Texians, they learned that Santa Anna had not yet come up. Houston took possession of a new boat which Santa Anna had forced some Americans to construct, and had it rowed up opposite the first grove on the Bayou. In the meantime, having arrived first, he could choose his own position, and he posted himself in a beautiful copse of trees which grew on a bend in the stream and lay in a semicircular form on the margin of the prairie. The trees and the undergrowth enabled him to conceal his forces on the bank of the river, and plant his artillery on the brow of the copse.

The Texian army was now ready to go into battle at a moment's warning. But as the enemy had not yet come up, they again lighted their fires to complete their culinary operations, which had been so suddenly interrupted a few hours previously. But they had scarcely laid aside their arms and kindled their fires, before Houston's scouts came flying into the camp with the news that the Mexicans were in sight—and shortly after Santa Anna's bugles were heard over the prairie, sounding the charge of the Mexican army.

Whatever may have been said to the contrary, it is perfectly certain that Santa Anna knew the position of the Texian General, and so far from his being surprised by a discharge from the Texian artillery, he intended to surprise the enemy himself. Accordingly he opened his "brass twelve-pounder" upon the Texian position, intending to sustain the artillery by his infantry and cavalry. But a well directed fire of grape-shot and canister from Houston's two six-pounders drove back the infantry column, which took shelter in a piece of timber within rifle shot of the, left wing of the Texian army. In the meantime the Mexican field-piece was kept playing, but with no other result than that Col. Neill, the gallant officer of the artillery, received a grape-shot in his thigh, which disabled him from service. These events took place about ten o'clock in the morning. Col. Sherman, of the 2d Regiment, requested of the commander permission, with a detachment, to drive the infantry from their covert. Houston, who had already decided (for reasons known then only to himself, but apparent enough the next day) his plan and time for action, complied with Col. Sherman's request, although he gave him positive orders not to advance beyond the piece of timber, or endanger the safety of his men. Houston directed him to take two companies of his regiment. He preferred charging on horseback. Houston gratified him. He was repulsed, and the circumstance produced no good effect upon the men.

General Houston, as appears from his dispatch, which we have already given, was resolved to choose his own time for fighting, and compensate for his want of numbers, by military skill and superior advantage in position. In other words, he was resolved to watch his opportunity and "fight the enemy to such advantage as would insure victory, though the odds were greatly against him."

Some slight skirmishing followed, which ended in Santa Anna's retiring with his army to a swell in the prairie, with timber and water in his rear. His position was near the bank of the Bay of San Jacinto, about three-quarters of a mile from the Texian camp, where he commenced a fortification.

Houston was well satisfied with the business of the day; and he declared to one of his confidential officers that evening, that, although he did not doubt he would that day have won a victory, if he had pursued the enemy, yet it would have been attended with a heavy loss of men—"while, tomorrow," says he, "I will conquer, slaughter, and put to flight the entire Mexican army—and it shall not cost me a dozen of my brave men." Those who clamored then, and have clamored since, about Houston's losing so fine an opportunity of fighting on the day before the Battle of San Jacinto, were, without doubt, brave men—but if they could have had their way at any one time after Houston took the command at Gonzales, it is more than certain it would have cost another Alamo or Goliad tragedy, and the day of San Jacinto would never have come.

Evening came on, and Houston was about to withdraw his army from the field, to give them time enough for refreshment and repose, and to prepare for the following day. The flight of the enemy in the first instance, and Santa Anna's rather precipitate retreat afterwards, had inspirited the Texian army. But Col. Sherman, who was determined to resort to a ruse for the purpose of forcing General Houston into a general engagement that day—now pressed the general most earnestly for leave to advance with his cavalry, and attempt the capture of the Mexican field-piece. Houston discountenanced the movement altogether—for he felt sure that his plan of giving battle to the enemy the next day would succeed, and he was reluctant to peril unnecessarily the life of a single man. He also had some reason to apprehend a similar result to that which followed Sherman's ill-advised movement that morning. But he importuned him till the general consented he might go out with the cavalry and *reconnoiter* the enemy's position and forces; but he peremptorily ordered him by no means to go within gun-shot of the enemy, nor court a conflict.

Houston ordered out the artillery and the infantry battalion behind an island of timber, to remain concealed, and if the enemy should attack Sherman's command, to be in readiness to meet and check their advance. Sherman disappeared with his cavalry behind the timber the enemy had occupied in the morning, and Houston and his staff awaited the result, utterly ignorant of the *ruse* of Sherman to force the Texian commander into a general engagement, and therefore unconscious of their imminent peril. The reconnoitering party had hardly disappeared, before the sound of firing in that direction was heard. In a single moment a suspicion of Sherman's *real* design flashed over Houston's mind; he mounted his horse and rode straight to the scene of action. He met Col. Sherman coming in. Although he had *not* succeeded in periling the entire army by forcing them into a general engagement, yet he had succeeded in sacrificing the life of the brave Trask, and disabling the intrepid Woodliff, both of whom were now being borne back. Houston was incensed, for all this had been done in direct violation of his orders, and two of his Spartan soldiers borne bleeding by, were the only fruits that had followed. Gen. Foote's History (vol. ii., p. 301) declares that this was "a bold and well-conceived *ruse* to delude the Commander-in-Chief into a conflict in spite of the monitions of his cooler judgment," though Sherman has since had the effrontery to declare that Gen. Houston sent him to be *cut off!* This would seem rather a singular charge, without remembering the circumstances, since Houston had lost neither a man nor a beast in his retreat to the Brazos, or in his advance to San Jacinto; and on the night before the battle, he certainly had no men to spare. We only allude to the circumstance, however, as a fair sample of the countless calumnies which disappointed and factious men have heaped upon the name of Houston. The best way to kill falsehood is to publish plain truth—and we shall not trouble ourselves to deny in detail the thousand and one false statements which have been published against the Texas Senator.

The Texian army now retired to their camp, and refreshed themselves for the first time in two days. "The enemy in the meantime extended the right flank of their infantry, so as to occupy the extreme point of a skirt of timber on the bank of the San Jacinto, and secured their left by a fortification about five feet high, constructed of packs and baggage, leaving an opening in the center of their breastwork in which their artillery was placed—the cavalry upon the left wing." (Extract from Gen. H.'s official report.)

Such was the position of the Mexican army, and they maintained it till the charge was made the next day.

CHAPTER VIII:

THE HERO OF SAN JACINTO

During the entire presence of the enemy, on the first day the hostile armies met, Houston had remained on horseback, exposed to their artillery, and served them as a target. Branches were cut down over his head by cannon balls, and one shot struck the bit of his horse's bridle. After he had doubled the vigilance of his encampment, to render surprise impossible, he was prevailed on by his staff to take some rest, for he had scarcely eaten or slept for several days. It was now evening twilight, and the men were enjoying a hasty repast of the beef they had found so difficult to cook.

Houston laid himself down under an old oak, with the coil of the artillery rope for his pillow. From the day he took command of the army, he had never been known to have one hour's sound rest. His only time of repose had been after four o'clock in the morning, when he beat three taps on the drum, which he had done every morning till that day. At four o'clock, the line was always formed, and every man kept under arms till daylight. He then lay down, and got what rest he could till the men had taken their breakfast, and were ready to march. In one of his letters to Mr. Rusk, during this period, in speaking of the solicitude he suffered, he says: "I will do the best I can; but be assured, the fame of Jackson could never compensate me for my anxiety and mental pain." All this suffering arose from uncertainty. He had expected troops and supplies, and waited for them in vain. The fall of the Alamo, and the massacre of Fannin's command, had dispirited his men, and caused desertions. The government itself had fled from the scene of danger, consternation had spread through Texas; he was in a new country, without the means of subsistence or transport; his men were but half clad and half armed; he was in the neighborhood of a powerful army, whose picket-guards outnumbered all the men in his camp, and he could decide neither the day nor the scene of battle. He had slept on the wet ground, without covering, his only dress was the garb of a hunter, and his food only kept him alive.

It is not strange, therefore, when the harrowings of suspense were over, and he, in the presence of the enemy, had posted his faithful guards and fixed his iron purpose, that this man could lie down and sleep calmly and profoundly throughout the entire night. But he was probably the only man in that camp over whose mind flitted no anxious vision.

The night which preceded the bloody slaughter of San Jacinto rolled anxiously away, and brightly broke forth the morning of the last day of Texian servitude. Before the first grey lines shot up the east, three strange taps of a drum were heard in the camp, and 700 soldiers sprang to their feet as one man. The camp was busy with the soldier-hum of preparation for battle, but in the midst of it all, Houston slept on calmly and profoundly. The soldiers had eaten the last meal they were to eat till they had won their independence. They were under arms, ready for the struggle.

At last the glorious sun came up over the prairie, without a single cloud. It shone full and clear in the face of the hero, and it waked him to battle. He sprang to his feet, and exclaimed, "the sun of Austerlitz has risen again." His face was calm, and for the first time in many weeks, every shade of trouble had moved away from his brow. He ordered his Commissary General, Col. John Forbes, to provide two good axes, and then sent for Deaf Smith. He took this faithful and intrepid man aside, and ordered him to conceal the axes in a safe place nearby, where he could lay his hands on them at a moment's warning, and not to pass the lines of the sentinels that day without his special orders, nor to be out of his call.

Morning wore away, and about nine o'clock, a large body of men was seen moving over a swell of the prairie in the direction of Santa Anna's camp. They were believed to be a powerful force which had come to join the Mexicans, and the spectacle produced no little excitement in the Texian lines. Houston saw it at a glance, and quelled the apprehension by coolly remarking, that "they were the same men they had seen the day before—they had marched round the swell in the prairie and returned in sight of the Texian camp to alarm their foe, with the appearance of an immense reinforcement—for it was very evident Santa Anna did not wish to fight. But it was all a *ruse de guerre* that could be easily seen through—a *mere Mexican trick."*

All this did very well, and yet Houston, of course, had quite a different notion on the subject. He sent Deaf Smith and a comrade with confidential orders as spies on their rearward march. They soon returned, and reported publicly that "the General was right—it was all a humbug." A few minutes after, Deaf Smith whispered quite another story in the private ear of the commander. The enemy seen was a reinforcement of 540 men, under Gen. Cos, who had heard Santa Anna's cannon the day before on the Brazos, and come on by forced marches to join his standard. But the secret was kept till it did no harm to reveal it. A proposition was made to the general to construct a floating bridge over Buffalo Bayou, "which might be used in the event of danger." Houston ordered his Adjutant and Inspector Generals and an aide to ascertain if the necessary materials could be obtained. They reported that by tearing down a house in the neighborhood, they could. "We will postpone it awhile at all events," was Houston's reply.

In the meantime, he had ordered Deaf Smith to report to him, with a companion, well mounted. He retired with them to the spot where the axes had been deposited in the morning. Taking one in either hand, and examining them carefully, he handed them to the two trusty fellows, saying, "Now, my friends, take these axes, mount, and make the best of your way to Vince's bridge; cut it down, and burn it up, and come back like eagles, or you will be too late for the day." This was the bridge over which both armies had crossed in their march to the battleground of San Jacinto, and it cut off all chance of escape for the vanquished. "This," said Deaf Smith, in his droll way, "looks a good deal like fight, General."

The reader will not fail to notice the difference between Houston's calculations of the results of that day, and those of some of his officers. *They* bethought themselves of building a *new* bridge—*he* of cutting down and burning up the only bridge in the neighborhood. The fact was, Houston was determined his army should come off victorious that day or leave their bodies on the field.

The day was now wearing away; it was three o'clock in the afternoon, and yet the enemy kept concealed behind his breastworks, and manifested no disposition to come to an engagement. Events had taken just such a current as Houston expected and desired, and he began to prepare for battle.

In describing his plan of attack, we borrow the language of his official report, after the battle was over. "The 1st Regiment, commanded by Col. Burleson, was assigned the center. The 2d Regiment, under the command of Col. Sherman, formed the left wing of the army. The artillery, under the special command of Col. George W. Hockley, Inspector-General, was placed on the right of the 1st Regiment, and four companies of infantry, under the command of Lieut. Col. Henry Millard, sustained the artillery upon the right. Our cavalry, sixty-one in number, commanded by Col. Mirabeau B. Lamar, placed on our extreme right, completed our line. Our cavalry was first dispatched to the front of the enemy's left, for the purpose of attracting their notice, whilst an extensive island of timber afforded us an opportunity of concentrating our forces and displaying from that point, agreeably to the previous design of the troops. Every evolution was performed with alacrity, the whole advancing rapidly in line, and through an open prairie, without any protection whatever for our men. The artillery advanced and took station within two hundred yards of the enemy's breastwork."

Those who expect a minute and accurate account of this engagement from the writer or anyone else must be disappointed, for no such description can ever be written. It was a *slaughter* more than a *battle*. We can only give the reader, with the aid of an illustration, a perfect idea of the position of both armies when the engagement began,—fill up the interval of the next few minutes with blood and smoke and cries and slaughter, and then tell the almost incredible result. The two armies were now drawn up in complete order. There were 700 Texians on the field, and Santa Anna's troops numbered *over eighteen hundred*. Houston had informed Mr. Rusk of the plan of the battle, and he approved of it as perfect. The Secretary, it is true, had never been a soldier—he understood little of military evolutions or the discipline of an army—but Houston knew he carried a lion-heart in his bosom, and he assigned him the command of the left wing. The general of course led the center.

Everything was now ready, and every man at his post waiting for the charge. The two six-pounders had commenced a well directed fire of grape and canister, and they shattered bones and baggage where they struck. The moment had at last come. Houston ordered the charge and sounded out the war cry, Remember the Alamo. These magic words struck the ear of every soldier at the same instant, and *the Alamo! the Alamo!* went up from the army in one wild scream, which sent terror through the Mexican host. At that moment a rider came up on a horse covered with mire and foam, swinging an axe over his head, and dashed along the Texian lines, crying out, as he had been instructed to do, *"I have cut down Vince's bridge—now fight for your lives and remember the* Alamo,*"*—and then the solid phalanx which had been held back for a moment at the announcement, launched forward upon the breastworks like an avalanche of fire. Houston spurred his horse on at the head of the center column right into the face of the foe.

The Mexican army was drawn up in perfect order, ready to receive the attack, and when the Texians were within about sixty paces, and before they had fired a rifle, a general flash was seen along the Mexican lines and a storm of bullets went rushing over the Texian army. They fired too high—several balls struck Houston's horse in the breast, and one ball shattered the general's ankle. The noble animal staggered for a moment, but Houston spurred him on. If the first discharge of the Mexicans had been well directed, it would have thinned the Texian ranks. But they pressed on, reserving their fire till each man could choose some particular soldier for his target, and before the Mexicans could reload, a murderous discharge of rifle balls was poured into their very bosoms. The Texian soldiers rushed on. They were without bayonets, but they converted their rifles into war-clubs and leveled them upon the heads of Santa Anna's men. Along the breastwork there was little more firing of muskets or rifles—it was a desperate struggle hand to hand. The Texians, when they had broken off their rifles at the breech by smashing in the skulls of their enemies, flung them down and drew their pistols. They fired them once; and having no time to reload, hurled them against the heads of their foes, and then drawing forth their bowie-knives, literally cut their way through dense masses of living flesh.

It would be a sad mistake to suppose that the Mexicans played the coward that day—for they were slain by hundreds in the ranks where they stood when the battle began—but the fierce vengeance of the Texians could not be resisted. They fought as none but freemen can fight, when they are striking for their homes, their families, and their dead kindred. The Mexican officers and men stood firm for a time, but the Texians stamped on them as fast as they fell, and trampled the prostrate and the dying down with the dead, and clambering over the groaning, bleeding mass, plunged their knives into the bosoms of those in the rear. When they saw, that the dreadful onset of their foe could not be resisted, they either attempted to fly, and were stabbed in the back or fell on their knees to plead for mercy, crying, *"me no Alamo!" "me no Alamo!" "me no Alamo!"* These unfortunate slaves of the Mexican tyrant had witnessed that brutal massacre of brave men, and now they could think of no other claim for mercy, but the plea they were not there, for they knew the day of vengeance for the Alamo had at last come.

But before the center breastwork had been carried, the right and left wing of the enemy had been put to the rout or the slaughter. The Mexicans, however, not only stood their ground at first, but made several bold charges upon the Texian lines.

A division of their infantry, of more than five hundred men, made a gallant charge, in handsome order, upon the battalion of Texian infantry. Seeing them hard pressed, by a force of three to one, the commander-in-chief dashed between them and the enemy's column, exclaiming—"Come on, my brave fellows, your General leads you." The battalion halted and wheeled into perfect order, like a veteran corps, and Houston gave the order to fire. If the guns of the Texians had all been moved by machinery they could not have been fired nearer the same instant. There was a single explosion;—the battalion rushed through the smoke, and those who had not been mowed down by the bullets were struck down by the cleaving blows of uplifted rifles; and the prostrate column were trampled into the mire together. Of the five hundred, only thirty-two lived, even to surrender as prisoners of war.

In the meantime, although Houston's wound was bleeding profusely, and his dying horse could scarce stagger his way over the slain, yet the commander-in-chief saw every movement of his army, and followed the tide of battle as it rolled over the field. Wherever his eye fell he saw the Mexicans staggering back under the resistless shock of his heroic soldiers. Regiments and battalions, cavalry and infantry, horses and men, were hurled together, and every officer and every man seemed to be bent upon a work of slaughter for himself.

The Mexican army had now been driven from their position, and were flying before their pursuers. Houston saw that the battle was won, and he rode over the field and gave his orders to stop the carnage of the wounded, and those who surrendered. But it would have been easier to stop the in-rolling tide of the sea. He had given the *Alamo* for their war-cry, and the magic word could not be recalled. The ghosts of brave men, massacred at Goliad and the Alamo, flitted through the smoke of battle, and the uplifted hand could not be stayed.

"While the battle was in progress," says General Rusk, "the celebrated Deaf Smith, although on horseback, fighting, was with the infantry. When they got pretty near the enemy, Smith galloped on ahead, and dashed directly up to the Mexican line. Just as he reached it, his horse stumbled and fell, throwing him on his head among the enemy. Having dropped his sword in the fall, he drew one of his belt-pistols, presented it at the head of a Mexican, who was attempting to bayonet him, and it missed fire. Smith then hurled the pistol itself at the head of the Mexican, and, as he staggered back, he seized his gun, and began his work of destruction. A young man, by the name of Robbins, dropped his gun in the confusion of the battle, and happening to run directly in contact with a Mexican soldier who had also lost his musket, the Mexican seized Robbins, and both being stout men, rolled to the ground. But Robbins drew out his Bowie knife, and ended the contest by cutting the Mexican's throat. On starting out from our camp, to enter upon the attack, I saw an old man, by the name of Curtis, carrying *two* guns. I asked him what reason he had for carrying more than one gun. He answered: 'Damn the Mexicans; they killed my son and son-in-law in the Alamo, and I intend to kill two of them for it, or be killed myself.' I saw the old man again during the fight, and he told me 'he had killed his two men; and if he could find Santa Anna himself he would cut out *a razor-strap from his back.*' "

Such was the day of vengeance. It was not strange that no invading army, however brave, could long withstand so dreadful an onset. "When the Mexicans were first driven from the point of woods where we encountered them," continues General Rusk, "their officers tried to rally them, but the men cried, 'It's no use, it's no use, there are a thousand Americans in the woods.' When Santa Anna saw Almonte's Division running past him, he called a drummer, and ordered him to beat his drum. The drummer held up his hands and told him he was shot. He called then to a trumpeter near him to sound his horn. The trumpeter replied that he, also, was shot. Just at that instant a ball from one of our cannon struck a man who was standing near Santa Anna, taking off one side of his head. Santa Anna then exclaimed, 'Damn these Americans; I believe they will shoot us all.' He immediately mounted his horse, and commenced his flight."

The flight had now become universal. The Texians had left on the ground, where the battle began, more than their entire number, dying and dead; and far away over the prairie they were chasing the flying, and following up the slaughter. Multitudes were overtaken and killed as they were making their escape through the deep grass. The Mexican cavalry were well mounted, and after the event they struck deep their spurs into their fleet horses, and turned their heads towards Vince's Bridge. They were hotly pursued by the victors, and when the latter came up, the most appalling spectacle, perhaps, of the entire day, was witnessed. When the fugitive horsemen saw that the bridge was gone, some of them, in their desperation, spurred their horses down the steep bank; others dismounted and plunged into the stream; some were entangled in their trappings, and were dragged down with their struggling steeds; others sunk at once to the bottom; while those whose horses reached the opposite bank fell backwards into the river. In the meantime, while they were struggling with the flood, their pursuers, who had come up, were pouring down upon them a deadly fire, which cut off all escape. Horses and men, by hundreds, rolled down together; the waters were red with their blood, and filled with their dying gurgles. The deep, turbid stream, was literally choked with the dead!

A similar spectacle was witnessed on the southern verge of the Island of Trees, near the Mexican encampment, in the rear of the battleground. There was little chance of escape in this quarter, for a deep morass was to be passed, and yet multitudes, in their desperation, had rushed to this spot as a forlorn hope. They had plunged into the mire and water with horses and mules, and, in attempting to pass, had been completely submerged; every one who seemed likely to escape soon received a ball from the murderous aim of a practiced rifleman, and the morass was literally bridged over with carcasses of dead mules, horses, and men.

But a company of about two hundred and fifty cooler or braver men had rallied in the Island of Trees, under Almonte, prepared to resist or surrender rather than fly. Houston rallied as large a body of men as could be assembled, and was preparing to lead them to the charge, when his gallant horse, that had so nobly borne his rider through the carnage of the battle, with seven balls in his body, at last staggered and fell dead. Houston, in dismounting, struck upon his wounded leg and fell to the earth. It was now discovered, for the first time, that he was wounded. Alarm immediately spread over the field. Houston called for General Rusk and gave him the command. He was then helped upon another horse by the officers of his staff, and General Rusk advanced with his newly-formed company upon the last remnant of the Mexican Army. Its commander, however, came promptly forward and surrendered his sword. Houston then cast a glance over the field and said, "I think now, gentlemen, we are likely to have no more trouble today, and I believe I will return to the Camp."

The party then rode slowly off from the field of victory and the resting place of the dead, and returned to the oak, at whose

foot the hero of San Jacinto had slept till the "Sun of Austerlitz" had woke him that morning. All resistance to the arms
of Texas ceased. The pursuers returned to the camp, where a
command was left to guard the spoils taken from the enemy. As
the commander-in-chief was riding across the field the victorious soldiers came up in crowds, and slapping him rudely on
his wounded leg, exclaimed—"Now, aren't we brave fellows,
General?" "Yes, boys, you have covered yourselves with glory,
and I decree to you the spoils of victory; I will reward valor. I
only claim to share the *honors* of our triumph with you."

While he was giving his orders, after he reached the Texian
encampment, and before he dismounted, General Rusk came
in and presented his prisoner Almonte. It was the first time
they had ever met. This seemed to give a finishing stroke to
the victory, and Houston, who was completely exhausted from
fatigue and loss of blood, fainted and fell from his horse. Colonel Hockley caught him in his arms, and laid him at the foot
of the oak.

Thus ended the bloody day of San Jacinto—a battle that
has scarcely a parallel in the annals of war. Its *immediate fruits*
were not small—for the spoils were of great value to men who
had nothing in the morning but the arms they carried, scanty,
coarse clothing, and the determination to be free. About 900
stand of English muskets (besides a vast number that were lost
in the morass and bayou), 300 sabres, and 200 pistols, 300
valuable mules, a hundred fine horses, a good lot of provisions,
clothing, tents, and paraphernalia for officers and men, and
twelve thousand dollars in silver, constituted the *principal* spoils.

But the booty was esteemed meaner than nothing, in comparison with the great moral and political consequences that
attended the victory. On that well-fought field Texian independence was won. A brave, but an outraged people, in imita-
tion of their fathers of the last age, had entrusted their cause
to the adjudication of battle, and God took care of the issue.
For my own part, I can find in the whole range of history no

spectacle more sublime. It was not a struggle for the aggrandizement of some military chieftain—nor was it a strife for empire—the soldiers, who marched under the "Lone Star" into that engagement, were free, brave, self-relying men. Some of them, indeed, had come from a neighboring Republic, as Lafayette crossed the sea, to join in the struggles of freedom, but most of the Texian army were men who cultivated the soil they fought on, and had paid for it with their money or their labor. Hundreds of them had abandoned their fugitive wives to achieve everlasting freedom for their children. They were fighting for all that makes life worth having, or gives value to its possessions.

And when the victors laid themselves down to rest that night, and Heaven folded its blue curtains kindly around them, and they thought that their troubles and anxieties were over—that they could now return to the embrace of their happy families with the hope of a long and peaceful life of earnest and manly endeavor, and a quiet old age, when they should hold their grandchildren on their knee, and tell them the story of the bloody day of San Jacinto—it is not strange that they felt more than compensated for all their privations and all their sufferings.

But the sublimity of the spectacle is lost unless the eye has scope for a wider field of vision. There *are* events whose consequences can be measured by no estimate into whose calculation *centuries* do not come. If the historian of the Plymouth colony could have lived a century longer, he might have perceived clearly what is now reduced only to a question of time, that from the day the Mayflower swung round to her mooring on the rock of Plymouth, the sceptre or the New World passed forever into the nervous hand of the Anglo-Saxon race. But for a long period this grand result seemed impossible, and he who should have proclaimed that it would one day take place, would have been called a dreamer. Spain and Portugal, France and England, had divided the Northern and Southern Hemisphere or the new found World. But the French empire in America received a fatal shock when England wrested from it the Canadas in 1763; and she afterwards lost by diplomacy what could not be wrested from her in battle.—*One dominion then disappeared.*

At last, when it became apparent that even Englishmen in America could not develop their strength under British sway, the drama of '76 began, and all that was valuable in the New Continent that belonged to England, became the heritage of her American children. *This was the second great act.*

In the meantime the powerful savage tribes, whose wigwams served as beacon fires to the earliest voyagers along the Atlantic coast, melted away before the steady advance of European population, and the *Indian dominion passed away.*

At last, the American people, *this new form of humanity*—which concentrated in itself nearly all those qualities, which, in past times, had given empire to separate nations, began to cross the frontiers of that ancient power which, for three hundred years, had made the fair valley of the Montezumas the seat of their dominion. But this began in *no encroachment—no invasion upon the rights or soil of a neighboring state.* Mexico, although she had caught enough of the all-pervading spirit of the Anglo-Saxon to rise and shake off the foul mantle of Spanish despotism, had not vital energy enough left within herself to work out her own political regeneration. She had been too long bowed into the dust by the foreign tyrant—she had been too long steeped in the besotted bigotry of superstition—she had never thought or acted for herself—she had no clear perception of human rights—no intelligent idea of liberty. She did not know that a nation never can grow rich by abandoning the cultivation of the soil, and digging gold and silver from the mine—she could not understand why it was that six vigorous republics had grown up into power on the cold barren hills of New England, while she had become feeble and impoverished in the midst of the very garden of the world. And yet she believed, if she could once introduce that northern population into her limits, she could borrow from them the secret of their magic power. Her statesmen were told that New Englanders, when they found they could not get their bread from their rocky, frozen soil, made commerce of stones and grew rich by exporting their granite, and lime, and cobblestones, during the summer, and sent off ship-loads of their surplus water as soon as it froze in winter, albeit they had to find their market for it on the other side of the globe. These, said the Mexican statesmen, are the men we must get to colonize our vast garden province of Texas—for we have for three centuries tried in vain to do it ourselves.

So that fertile territory was thrown open to the people of the United States, and they were plied with all those motives of gain and pledges of protection which, in the mind of the pioneer settler, prove too strong for the allurements of home. A band of choice spirits—hardy, working men, who had been trained in the district schools of New York and New England, and cultivated their cold, ungrateful soil—were led out to find their new homes in the fair province of New Estramadura, where all nature was blushing under the purple light of the tropics. At their head went STEPHEN F. AUSTIN; one of those few men upon whose incorruptible, dauntless truth, a young nation finds it her salvation to repose. In his rare and great character, all that was lofty in the Cavalier and uncompromising in the Puritan was mingled.

He entered into his obligations with the Mexican government, and conducted all his negotiations and redeemed all his pledges, in good faith. For a time, Mexico stood by her engagements, and the infant colony struck its roots deep into the soil. At last Mexico discovered that the very qualities from which she promised herself so much advantage—the industry, the enterprise, the inventions of the new colonists, were all owing to that intelligent love of liberty which she so little understood, and yet so much dreaded. She saw that men who had energy enough to be good settlers, where Spaniards had failed, had too much independence ever to be governed as Spaniards. But she found out her mistake only when it was too late to correct it. Like the ancient Briton, she had invited a superior race into her country, unconscious that her sceptre would one day be transferred to their hands.

This was the point upon which the destiny of the old Spanish empire hinged. Mexico might now have borrowed from her new subjects the elements of an entire political regeneration. These colonists were not ambitious men—they went there *only to cultivate the soil*—but they had carried, of necessity, their civilization and love of liberty with them, and they could not brook the tyranny of Mexican dictators. They went prepared to stand by the Federal Constitution of 1824, and up to the 2nd of March, 1836, when the Declaration of Independence was signed, all the protests and discontents, all the demands and petitions of the Texians were *limited to a concession of the rights secured to all the States by that Constitution!*

But Mexico was now under the sway of selfish, ambitious military chieftains, who, in the struggle for supremacy, had trampled the Constitution of1824 into the dust. And let it never be forgotten, that when the political agitations of Texas began, and the will of the entire people had been declared, *all they asked for, and all they desired then, was to see the Constitution of 1824 preserved inviolate.* But men who are driven to the wall and compelled to fight for life, sometimes fight for victory. Mr. Austin was then Commissioner to Mexico, and he went to the capital with his memorial. His very appearance in that city with the prayer of his colony, that the Mexicans would abide by their own constitution, under whose solemn pledges he had led his people to their new home—was too bitter a sarcasm upon the corrupt tyrants who had trampled down that high compact, and he was plunged into a foul dungeon, where for many months he never saw a beam of sunshine, nor even the hand that fed him.

How was all this tampering with Anglo-Saxon men to end? Who, that knows what plighted faith means, or has any notion of the obligations growing out of a political compact, will pretend to say that Texas was bound to submit to the decrees of a dictator who had committed high treason against his government—treason for which he would have been brought to the block by the people of Mexico, had he not had 20,000 bayonets at his back. The Federal compact had now been broken, and by the highest law of nations, every state of the Union not only had the right, but was bound in duty to take care of itself. *An immediate* Declaration of Independence would have been justified by the world. But Texas still remonstrated, and still prayed. *All she wanted, was a return to the Constitution of 1824.* But that Constitution lay bleeding under the hoofs of Santa Anna's battle horse, and his myrmidon soldiers had possession of the capital. War was proclaimed against Texas by Mexico, because she would not acknowledge a Dictator;—and an invading army was sent across the Rio Grande, to *"lay waste the infant colony, and slaughter all its inhabitants."*

This was the position of Texas—and if those men were not justified in defending their wives and children from slaughter, and their dwellings from fire, there never was a people who had a right to smite the arm of a tyrant. The heroes of '76 rebelled against a constitutional government, with its parliament and king, because they were required to pay a stamp tax. *The Texians never rebelled at all.* They would not bow to a dictator who had stamped the free constitution of his country under his feet;—and now a war of extermination was proclaimed. Seven hundred brave men were slaughtered and burned to ashes, after they had, under a solemn pledge that their lives should be spared, surrendered themselves prisoners of war.

The red flame of exterminating war was now rolling over the very bosom of the young republic, whose only crime was her loyalty to the Federal Constitution!

At last the slaughter-day of San Jacinto came, and the Texians who went into battle knew that every one of them would have been put to death in cold blood, if the enemy had conquered. Such had been the case at Goliad and the Alamo, and such was the watch-word of the advancing dictator. But high over the smoke and screams of the field of San Jacinto, I seem to see, and I do see, the hand of the God of Freedom and of Vengeance. His purposes were unknown to man, but they could not be overthrown. The wing of his Almighty Providence had sheltered the bark of the Pilgrims, and his strong arm had been thrown around the rude homes of Plymouth. Over the deliberations of the Provincial Congress He again presided, and in the Declaration of Independence His will was done. And now, having decreed, that the broad prairies and shining rivers of that vast land, which had groaned under the tramp of despotic power, and been blasted by the withering blight of superstition for ages, should be regenerated by a nobler and better race, He had begun to reveal his great purposes.

The *last* act of this drama, which had begun on the shores of New England, was to be opened on the field of San Jacinto. And although the sun gleamed on the armor of more than eighteen hundred men that morning, and when the commander's bugles sounded the charge, he was, to all human appearances, sure of a victory; yet the result proved that the battle is not always to the strong—that "God rules among the nations of the earth, and giveth its kingdoms lavishly to whomsoever He will." A decree had gone forth against that army, and against the sceptre of Spanish power in Mexico—" thy dominion is taken from thee."

And the future historian will, one day, open his scroll by announcing that when the sun went down over the groans and the slaughter of San Jacinto, the dominion of Mexico passed forever away. Such had been the first four acts of the drama of the New World.

> *The Fifth, then closed the Drama with the day,*
> *Time's noblest offspring was the last.*

CHAPTER IX:
THE VICTOR & THE CAPTIVE

The battle of independence had been fought. Seven hundred soldiers had met nearly three times their number, and come off victorious. Six hundred and thirty men were left dead on the field; among them were one general officer, four colonels, two lieutenant-colonels, seven captains, and twelve lieutenants. Multitudes had perished in the morass and the bayous. Of the surviving, upwards of two hundred and eighty were wounded, and there were nearly eight hundred prisoners. Only seven men are known to have escaped from the field. And yet, incredible as it may seem, this bloody engagement had cost the Texians the lives of only seven men, and less than thirty had been wounded. It was incredible, and when the commander-in-chief awoke the next morning, he asked, "Are we really victors, or is it only my dream?"

At ten o'clock in the morning, Gen. Houston sent a detachment of men to bury those who had fallen in battle; but decomposition had taken place so rapidly, the troops returned and reported they could not execute his order! This extraordinary circumstance excited the greatest surprise, and the Mexican prisoners accounted for it by resolving it, like the defeat of the previous day, into "a malignant blast of destiny."

In the meantime, a large number of Texians were scouring the prairie throughout the day, and bringing in prisoners. The grass was everywhere four or five feet high, and those who had not been taken the day before, were now crawling away on their hands and knees, hoping thus to effect their escape. Santa Anna had not yet been taken, but the victors were scouring over the field in search of the dictator. "You will find the Hero of Tampico," said Houston, "if you find him at all, making his retreat *on all fours*, and he will be dressed as bad at least as a common soldier. Examine every man you find, closely."

Lieutenant Sylvester, a volunteer of Cincinnati, was riding over the prairie, on a fine horse, about three o'clock in the afternoon, when he saw a man making his way towards Vince's bridge. The moment he saw he was pursued, the fugitive fell down in the grass. Sylvester dashed on in that direction, and his horse came very near trampling him down. The man sprang to his feet, and apparently without the slightest surprise, looked his captor full in the face. He was disguised in a miserable rustic dress. He wore a skin-cap, a round jacket, and pantaloons of blue domestic cotton, and a pair of coarse, soldier's shoes. But his face and his manners bespoke, too plainly, that he belonged to a different class than his garb betokened; and underneath his coarse disguise, Sylvester saw that he wore a shirt of the finest linen cambric. "You are an officer, I perceive, sir," said the horseman, raising his cap politely. "No, soldier," was his reply; and he drew out a letter in Spanish, addressed to Almonte. When he saw there was no hope of escape, he inquired for General Houston. By this time, Sylvester had been joined by several of his comrades, and mounting his prisoner behind him, they rode off together, on the same horse, to the camp, several miles distant. As he rode by the Mexican prisoners, they exclaimed with the greatest surprise as they lifted their caps, "El Presidente!"

In a single moment, the news spread through the camp that Gen. Santa Anna was a prisoner, and the dictator was taken to Houston. The general was lying on the ground, and having slept little during the night, in consequence of his wound, had now fallen into a doze. Santa Anna came up behind him, and took his hand. Houston roused himself, and turning over, gazed up in the face of the Mexican, who extended his left arm, and laying his right hand on his heart, said, *"I am General Antonio Lopez de Santa Anna, President of the Mexican Republic, and I claim to be your prisoner of war."* Houston waved his hand to a box, for it was the only seat in the camp, and asked his prisoner to be seated; and then sent for Almonte, who spoke English perfectly, requesting him to act as interpreter.

In the meantime, Santa Anna had taken his seat, and glancing his keen eye occasionally around the camp, with a timid expression, pressed the sides of his breasts with both hands, and gave two or three half-suppressed groans, like a man who was suffering deep pain. An interesting incident took place about this time, which is thus related by Gen. Rusk: "At the time Santa Anna was brought into our camp, I was walking with young Zavala. (The reader will recognize in this youthful character, the son of the noble and venerable Zavala, who distinguished himself as the friend of Texian independence.) We approached him together. Santa Anna recognized young Zavala at once, and advanced to meet him with great apparent cordiality, uttering many expressions of kindness, such as are customary among the Mexicans on such occasions, several of which I remember. Among other things, he exclaimed "Oh! my *friend*, my *friend*, the son of my *early* friend;" with which, and other exclamations in the same strain, he embraced young Zavala, with high indications of *apparent* feeling, and I think, *dropping a tear.* Young Zavala returned his greeting with that deference which would have been due to his former rank and power; but at the same time, emitting from his countenance an expression I have scarcely seen equaled on any occasion. His look seemed to wither Santa Anna, and staring him full in the face, he replied immediately, with great modesty, 'It has been so, sir.' Santa Anna evinced plainly that he was much mortified."

Almonte approached his captive general with evident respect and grief, and the following conversation took place between the two commanders; Houston, in the meantime, lying on the ground, resting on his elbow. Great pains have been taken to get as nearly as possible the exact words used by the speakers, and those who were present at the interview, have assured us, that all here related they do remember, and they recollect nothing else of importance.

Santa Anna (after embracing Almonte, and recovering perfectly from his embarrassment, rose, and advancing with the air of one born to command, said to General Houston—"That man may consider himself born to no common destiny, who has conquered the Napoleon of the West; and it now remains for him to be generous to the vanquished."

Houston—You should have remembered that at the Alamo.

S. A.—You must be aware that I was justified in my course by the usages of war. I had summoned a surrender, and they had refused. The place was then taken by storm, and the usages of war justified the slaughter of the vanquished.

H.—That was the case once, but it is now obsolete. Such usages among civilized nations have yielded to the influences of humanity.

S. A.—However this may be, I was acting under the orders of my government.

H.—Why, *you are the government of Mexico.*

S. A.—I have orders in my possession commanding me so to act.

H.—A dictator, sir, has no superior.

S. A.—I have orders, General Houston, from my government, commanding me to exterminate every man found in arms in the province of Texas, and treat all such as pirates; for they have no government, and are fighting under no recognized flag. This will account for the positive orders of my government.

H.—So far as the first point is concerned, the Texians flatter themselves they have a government already, and they will probably be able to make a flag. But if you feel excused for your conduct at San Antonio, you have not the same excuse for the massacre of Colonel Fannin's command. They had capitulated on terms proffered by your general. And yet after the capitulation they were all perfidiously massacred, without the privilege of even dying with arms in their hands.

Those who were present say that when Houston came to speak of the Goliad tragedy, it seemed impossible for him to restrain his indignation. His eye flashed like a wild beast's, and in his gigantic effort to curb in his wrath, cold sweat ran off from his brow in streams.

S. A.—I declare to you, General (laying his hand on his heart), that I was not apprised of the fact that they had capitulated. General Urrea informed me that he had conquered them in battle, and under this impression I ordered their execution.

H.—I *know*, General, that the men had capitulated.

S. A.—Then I was ignorant of it. And after your asseveration I should not have a shadow of doubt, if it were not that *General Urrea had no authority whatever to receive their capitulation.* And if the day ever comes that I can get Urrea into my hands, I will execute him for his duplicity in not giving me information of the facts.

Here the conversation was suspended for a while, and Santa Anna requested a small piece of opium. It was ordered by Houston, who asked him if he would desire his marquee and luggage, and the attendance of his aides and servants. Santa Anna thanked him very politely, and said "it would make him very happy, since they were proffered by his captor."

While the order was being given, Almonte manifested a disposition to continue the conversation with Houston. After remarking to the Texian General that fortune had indeed favored him, he asked why he had not attacked the Mexicans the first day the armies met. "You had reason to suppose we should be reinforced. And yet if you had risked a battle that day you would have had another story to tell, perhaps, for our men were then ready to fight, and so anxious for the battle to come on, that we could hardly keep them in their ranks. Why did you wait till the next morning, General?"

"Well," replied Houston, "I see I was right. I knew you expected I should bring on the battle that day, and were consequently prepared for it. Now if I must be questioned by an inferior officer in the presence of his General, I will say *that was just the reason why I did not fight*; and besides, I thought there was no use in having two bites at one cherry." After some remark of Almonte, which irritated Houston, and which, in the opinion of all who heard it, ill-befitted the occasion, he said—"You have come a great way to give us a great deal of trouble—and you have made the sacrifice of the lives of a great many brave men necessary." "Oh," flippantly replied Almonte, "what are six or eight hundred men! And, from all accounts, only half a dozen of your brave men have fallen."

Houston replied: "We estimate the lives of our men, I perceive, somewhat higher than you do," and gave him a look which seemed to say, "taunt me again, and you don't live an hour." Almonte very politely changed his tone. "You talk about reinforcements, sir," said Houston, raising himself up, "it matters not how many reinforcements you have, sir, you *never* can conquer freemen." And taking from his pocket an ear of dry corn which he had carried for four days, only a part of it being consumed, he held it up and said, "Sir, do you ever expect to conquer men who fight for freedom, whose general can march four days with one ear of corn for his rations?"

The exhibition of the ear of corn stirred up all the enthusiasm of the Texian soldiers, and they gathered round their general, and asked him to allow them to divide the corn. "We'll plant it," said they, "and call it the Houston corn." "Oh, yes, my brave fellows," said the general, smiling, "take it along if you care anything about it, and divide it among you—give each one a kernel as far as it will go, and take it home to your own fields, where I hope you may long cultivate the noble arts of peace as well as you have shown yourselves masters of the art of war. You have achieved your independence—now see if you cannot make as good farmers as you have proved yourselves gallant soldiers. You may not call it Houston corn; but call it *San Jacinto* corn—for then it will remind you of your own bravery." It is also said that in one of his dispatches that day to the people of the Sabine, the general said to those who had fled from their homes, "return and plant corn." The soldiers distributed their corn, and it now waves over a thousand green fields of the New Republic.

Santa Anna had become interested in the conversation, and Almonte related to him what had been said. The Mexican general seemed to be transported with rage, and he cursed Almonte for losing the battle. He was mortified beyond measure to think that his large army, perfectly armed and munitioned, with officers whose camp was filled with every luxury, should have been conquered by an undisciplined band of raw troops, incompletely armed, and whose officers were destitute of most even of the necessaries of life. It is worthy of remark, also, that Santa Anna afterwards said *"that this was the first moment he had ever understood the American character; and that what he had witnessed, convinced him that Americans never could be conquered."*

Santa Anna's marquee was set near the spot where Houston was lying. His trunks were not examined, nor any portion of his baggage molested. The Texian general knew that there was hardly a man in his army who did not wish to see Santa Anna expiate his crimes with his blood, and very few believed it would be possible even for Houston to protect him from assassination. But he knew the eyes of the civilized world would be turned upon the Texian camp, and that however guilty Santa Anna may have been, the name of Texas would be given over to execration if any violence was offered to the captive. He therefore took the necessary precautions to see that not only no violence but no indignity should be offered to his prisoner. The course he took in this matter entitles him to the regard of mankind. The feeling that prevailed in the army could not be mistaken, and various circumstances have come to our knowledge which serve to illustrate not only Houston's extreme vigilance, but his superior shrewdness in detecting insubordination, and his address in putting it down. One example we will allude to.

An officer had resolved to shoot Santa Anna, and had prepared himself for the work. His design, however, he had kept to himself, and Houston could have had no intimation of it from any quarter. But as the officer was passing Houston on the day of the night he had fixed on for the execution of his purpose, the general, who saw something wrong in his manner, beckoned him to approach. He conversed with him, privately and confidentially, on the subject of his fears, and after depicting the horrible consequences that would follow Santa Anna's assassination, told the officer that he had made him his confidant in the matter, because he knew he would be more likely than any other man in the camp to detect any murderous scheme projected, and he relied on his vigilance. The officer gave him his pledge he would act on his suggestion, and, moreover, declared that Santa Anna should never be assassinated while he stayed in the camp. He was as good as his word and yet he afterwards declared he had, at the very time, the arms on his person with which he had sworn to kill Santa Anna. Such was one of the thousand expedients Houston was obliged to resort to, to maintain discipline over those wayward, reckless men. No one knew how he did it, and yet it passed into a proverb that *Houston was the only man in the world that could have kept the army in subjection, or achieved the independence of Texas, or preserved it after it was won.* Houston, therefore, exercised the keenest vigilance over the safety of his prisoner, and treated him as a guest and a gentleman, rather than as a captive.

Night came—the guard was so disposed as to include Santa Anna's marquee, and he slept on his camp-bed with every comfort he could have had if he had been the victor; while, nearby him, Houston lay upon the earth—his wonted bed in camp—with no respite from the intense agony of his wound. The ball had entered about one inch above the ankle joint, shattering the bone, and severing the muscles and arteries. It prostrated him for months, during which time he was worn down by fever and pain to the shadow of a man.

On the evening of the day which followed the victory, two bald eagles were seen hovering over the field of battle, with their heads turned to the westward. Houston heard of the circumstance, and at the same time several practiced riflemen started to shoot them. He ordered them to be called back, saying, "Don't shoot them, comrades—their heads are turned towards the West—it is a good omen. The bird of Washington points out to you the course of your empire. I own I am a little superstitious." The riflemen came back and till late that night, the two birds beat their wings heavily over the field of the slain, with their heads pointing towards the going down of the sun.

The next morning Santa Anna asked leave to see General Houston, which was granted. He presented himself elegantly dressed in citizen's garb, and tendered a most respectful and cordial greeting to his "host," and inquired kindly for his health and the condition of his wound. The difference in the dresses of the two men was striking. Houston had on a plain, old, black coat, snuff-colored pantaloons, a black velvet vest, a fur cap, a worn out pair of boots, and a scimitar of tried metal, with a plated scabbard—a gift from his friend Captain Joseph Bonnell of Fort Jessup. He had worn it hung by buckskin thongs. This constituted his wardrobe and his armory. Santa Anna would have been taken for the victor, and Houston for the captive.

The Texian commander received, with courtesy, his prisoner, who immediately proposed negotiations for his liberty. Houston, *who, from the beginning to the end of Santa Anna's capture, never was alone with him a single moment,* immediately sent for the Secretary of War, who came, and they conversed some time with the prisoner. Santa Anna submitted a proposition written in pencil, and General Rusk had the paper translated. In the meantime General Houston informed the Mexican "President" that he could take no action on his proposals, as Texas was ruled by a constitutional government, whose members had been sent for immediately after the battle. Santa Anna naturally asked where the government was—a question which he found could not be so easily answered.

This "government" had, as we have already stated, fled from the scene of danger, and scattered to the four winds of Heaven. Fortunately, it was known where the head of the government was, or rather where he *had* been, for he had escaped to Galveston, and prepared to take passage on a little vessel called the *Flash*, before even the first flash of the enemy's guns. Houston thinking he might wait there till the news of the battle came, since even so *prudent* a man would perceive he could have plenty of time to get his craft under way before the victors could reach him, had dispatched his first express to that quarter.

Santa Anna, who had a great aversion against any negotiations with civilians, manifested a perfect willingness to act with military men. But Houston and Rusk were immovable in their determination. A detachment of 250 Texians was then ordered to march with a dispatch from Santa Anna, in which General Filisola was instructed to depart immediately, with all the Mexican troops, as far at least as Monterey, and this order had been tendered to General Houston without an intimation that even Santa Anna's life should be spared. Filisola was on the east side of the Brazos when he received news of the disaster of San Jacinto from an officer who had escaped from the battlefield on a fleet Andalusian courser, and succeeded in reaching his camp.

It was night when he reached Filisola's headquarters, and the camp broke up in confusion, and prepared for flight. They fired a large cotton gin, to have the benefit of the flames to light up their passage over the river. The Texian detachment pressed on by forced marches in pursuit of the rear-guard of the Mexican army. They found horses, and mules, and baggage-wagons, and sick soldiers, scattered along the path of the flying division, which indicated the utter consternation with which the retreat had been made. They had been obliged to march through a low, flat, wet prairie, in reaching the Colorado. But they were overtaken by the pursuers, and Filisola received the messengers who bore the flag with every mark of respect, and pledged himself to execute General Santa Anna's orders without any delay. He asked leave only to take some cattle along his march—he stretched his license far enough to rob every living thing he fell in with on his way. Filisola's division got under way, and the Texian detachment began their march back to San Jacinto.

Houston had given orders that a portion of the spoils should be divided equally among officers and men, and appointed three superior officers to execute his order.

A great number of incidents occurred during this period, which would serve to illustrate the character. But we are obliged to omit their relation. A soldier, for example, had fled from the battle, declaring that all his comrades were killed at the first fire. When General Houston heard of the circumstance, he declared he would have him shot. His captain importuned the commander to let him go. "Why, yes, Captain," said the general, "I will let him off, but on condition that he will promise to marry into a valiant race and cross the breed. On these conditions, I will let him go." The news of the victory spread by expresses all over the country, and not many days elapsed before the little steamboat *Yellow Stone* arrived from Galveston, bringing the (fugitive) "government;" and they boldly marched right into the very presence of Santa Anna himself! But when they came from their hiding places, they looked, of course, more like victors than fugitives. Houston, at once, surrendered everything into their hands but the money; this had been already divided among his gallant comrades.

Those who understand much of humanity will not be surprised to hear that, from that day forward, these "fugitive statesmen" became the irrevocable foes of the brave man who had redeemed the nation which they had deserted in the hour of her darkest trial. They had fled, and Houston had fought; they knew the odium that would rest upon their names, and as

Houston had been covered with the fame of a hero, they never could forgive him. An old philosopher once said, we never do forgive anybody whom we have injured. They did not express any aversion to, or condemnation of, Houston's acts—this would not have been particularly safe—but their future conduct showed most clearly, that, from that day, they were bent upon his destruction.

They began by treating him with manifest coolness. A proposition was even made to dismiss him from service, alleging no *cause*, but many *reasons*. Mr. Rusk, the Secretary of War, who, when the cabinet fled to the seashore, had fled to the camp, and toiled with its heroic soldiery, partaking of their privations and mingling in its perils—Mr. Rusk, the patriot-soldier, met the proposition in a spirited and indignant manner, and defeated their malicious machinations. The $12,000 had been distributed among the soldiers, and this was a crime heavy enough to damn Houston; for the "government" thought they needed it for their own purposes and it is quite likely they did. But the "government" did not dare to bring it forward as an accusation against the general, for they knew it would have roused the indignation of every man in the army.

The Secretary of War wrote a letter to Houston, asking his views about the release of Santa Anna. He returned the following answer:

HEADQUARTERS OF THE ARMY,
Camp San Jacinto, 3rd May, 1836.

I have not the pleasure to know on what basis the Executive Government contemplate the arrangement with General Santa Anna, but I would respectfully suggest, that so far as I have been enabled to give my attention to the subject, the following points should have some weight:

The recognition of the Independence of Texas should be a *sine qua non*. The limits of Texas should extend to the Rio Grande, and from the mouth, pursuing the stream to its most northwestern source, and from thence northeast to the line of the United States. Indemnity for all losses sustained by Texas during the war. Commissioners to be appointed for ascertaining the facts—one Mexican, one Texian, and one American. The guarantee to be obtained from the United States, for the fulfillment of the stipulation on the part of the contending parties. General Santa Anna to be retained as a hostage, with such other officers as the Government may think proper, until they are recognized or ratified by the Mexican Government. Immediate restoration of Texian or Mexican citizens, or those friendly to the cause of Texas, who may have been retained, with their property. Instantaneous withdrawal of all the Mexican troops from the limits of Texas. All property in Texas to be restored, and not molested by the troops or marauders in falling back. Cessation of all hostilities by sea and land. A guarantee for the safety and restoration of Mexican prisoners, so soon as the conditions shall be complied with. Agents to be sent to the United States to obtain the mediation of that government in the affairs of Mexico and Texas.

An attempt was made to heap upon Houston the odium both of Santa Anna's release and imprisonment after the treaty. But the attempt succeeded only for a time, as falsehood always will, and then these charges, with a thousand others, returned to plague the inventors. But in Texas they never were believed at all—there the facts were all known. It is a curious circumstance, that the report once so common in the United States, and even till now uncontradicted by Houston (for he never esteemed any lie worth contradicting), viz. that Houston played the coward at San Jacinto, and never would have fought at all if he had not been forced into battle by his soldiers; that he fled from the field, or—as many had it—was never in the field at all,—should have originated and been industriously circulated by the very men who had been the first to fly from danger, and leave the country in its darkest hour to take care of itself! And yet such was the case. But from all these "mountain lies" the name of Houston has come out fair and clear.

Volunteers had now rushed in from all quarters, where the news of the victory had gone; and some brave men, who had come on by forced marches to join Houston's standard when he needed their help, had the misfortune, also, to reach the camp too late. Great activity, discipline and vigor became necessary. Houston was rendered perfectly helpless by his wound and it was believed that, even if he survived, he would not be again fit for service for many months. He signified his desire that General Rusk should succeed him in the command, and, as no other man would have been acceptable, he was selected by the cabinet as Brigadier-General. From the arrival of the "government," which, to the surprise of Santa Anna, had at last been found, the Mexican President had not been permitted to pay his customary morning visit to his courteous and humane captor; and he had also been kept under the irritating and humiliating surveillance of the cabinet. This unnecessary and indelicate severity (or, as Santa Anna himself termed it, "bad manners") was a source of great pain and mortification to the captive general.

Mr. Lamar was appointed Secretary of War, to fill the vacancy in the cabinet. After the failure to disgrace Houston, there was a cruel effort made to depress and harrow his feelings. Every petty artifice was resorted to, to torture the feelings of the enfeebled, wounded hero. A fine stallion, that had been ridden in battle by Almonte, and captured by Karnes in the pursuit of the enemy, had been presented by that gallant officer to his general. Although the animal was not of the spoils taken on the field, Houston sent him to parade, and to be sold for the benefit of the army. By the united voice of the camp, he was led up to his master, with an earnest entreaty that he would retain him, and "they hoped, too," they said, "the General would be able to ride him very quickly." He was a noble animal; he was as black as a raven. After the army had confirmed the present of Karnes, the "government" took the horse from the commander. This was, certainly, a chivalrous act towards a man who had saved the country, and was yet unable to move, even on crutches. We will state one more circumstance about these men, and then leave them to the fame they are so sure to win with posterity, for having tortured the savior of his country.

When the army were taking up their line of march to the west, with the settlements all broken up, and Houston was without any of the comforts the wounded man so much needs, when his surgeon had no medicine in the camp to give him, or dress his wound with, and it became necessary for him to visit New Orleans as the nearest place he could go to for medical aid to save his life, and the steamboat was ready to sail for Galveston, with the cabinet, and Santa Anna and suite; these gentlemen had, by common consent, agreed to leave the wounded commander-in-chief to die—in sight of the field of San Jacinto! Houston could hardly believe this, and yet, when he saw he was going to be left in his helplessness, he applied to the cabinet for a passage. *The application was sternly refused!*

The captain of the boat, hearing of the circumstance, vowed his boat never should leave the shore without it bore General Houston, brought his hands up with him, and carried the wounded soldier aboard. He was also accompanied by a few of his staff; among others his surgeon-general, Dr. Ewing. When the doctor came on board, Mr. Lamar told him he could not accompany General Houston, and if he did, he would be discharged from the service. The surgeon told Houston of this. "I am sorry, my dear fellow," said he, "for I have nothing to promise you in the future, and you know I am poor; so you had better not incur the displeasure of the new Secretary of War." But the magnanimous man determined to follow his general, for he would not desert either a friend or a brave man in the hour of need. He went but the Secretary was as good as his word; he dismissed him at once from the army. He did not know then that Houston's star was so soon to come forth from its deep eclipse. When Santa Anna, who had wept when he was told that General Houston was not coming on board, saw him brought on, he ran to him, and embraced him with unfeigned joy.

The boat reached Galveston Island, where, at the time, there was not a framed house, and remained there for the night. Some volunteers, who had arrived there from the United States, hearing the President *ad interim*, when he went on shore, cast some reflections upon Houston, their officers immediately waited on the general, and offered to take him off, and do anything he might desire for his comfort or his honor. He was aware of the spirit the men felt, for they showed it too plainly to allow it to be mistaken, and he declined going just then. But he issued an order as he took leave of the men, and exhorted them to "render obedience to the authorities of the country, and not dishonor themselves by any disrespect to the government, being assured that by honoring the ranks they would be qualified for the highest rights of citizenship." They discussed the subject of treating the cabinet with great harshness; but they at last yielded to Houston's commands and entreaties, and smothered their indignation. A single word from the wounded man would have crushed those restless and ambitious men, who had inflicted so much pain upon himself, and afterwards brought so much misery and dishonor upon his country. But on this occasion, as on all others, he showed how well regard for law and order had fitted him to govern, and how easy it is for a truly great man to be magnanimous to his enemies.

We had nearly forgotten to mention the scene which was witnessed when Houston parted with the army. He was too feeble to speak to them, but he dictated the following touching address, which was read in camp as Army Orders.

Headquarters, San Jacinto, May 5th, 1836.

COMRADES—Circumstances connected with the battle of the 21st render our separation, for the present, unavoidable. I need not express to you the many painful sensations which that necessity inflicts upon me. I am solaced, however, by the hope, that we shall soon be reunited in the great cause of Liberty. Brigadier-General Rusk is appointed to command the army for the present. I confide in his valor, his patriotism, his wisdom. His conduct in the battle of San Jacinto was sufficient to ensure your confidence and regard.

The enemy, though retreating, are still within the limits of Texas; their situation being known to you, you cannot be taken by surprise. Discipline and subordination will render you invincible. Your valor and heroism have proved you unrivaled. Let not contempt for the enemy throw you off your guard. Vigilance is the first duty of a soldier, and glory the proudest reward of his toils.

You have patiently endured privations, hardships, and difficulties unparalleled; you have encountered odds of two to one of the enemy against you, and borne yourselves, in the onset and conflict of battle, in a manner unknown in the annals of modern warfare. While an enemy to your independence remains in Texas, the work is incomplete; but when liberty is firmly established by your patience and your valor, it will be fame enough to say, "I was a member of the army of San Jacinto."

In taking leave of my brave comrades in arms, I cannot suppress the expression of that pride which I so justly feel in having had the honor to command them in person, nor will I withhold the tribute of my warmest admiration and gratitude for the promptness with which my orders were executed, and union maintained through the army. At parting, my heart embraces you with gratitude and affection.

SAM HOUSTON,
COMMANDER-IN-CHIEF.

It is said that when this touching and eloquent address was read to the army, the tears of the brave men fell upon the rifles on which they were leaning. Such was his parting with his companions in arms.

A small war vessel, belonging to the Republic, was sailing from Galveston to New Orleans. Houston applied for a passage with his staff. It was refused! A little American schooner (the *Flora*) was also lying there, bound for the same port. The general sent for the captain, and contracted with him for himself and staff, to be paid when he could, for he had not a dollar of money to advance. During the entire campaign, neither he nor any one of his followers had received a shilling from the "government," and all the funds he had of his own, he had generously devoted to the relief of the fugitive women and children, whose husbands and fathers had been slaughtered at the Alamo, or massacred with Fannin. Santa Anna now asked permission of the cabinet to take leave of General Houston, but he was refused that privilege. Captain Chas. Hawkins, of the Texian Navy, stated these facts; and he also said, that Santa Anna wept on the occasion.

We pass over the long and tedious voyage of the little schooner. She arrived at the Balize in the night, and the next day was towed up to New Orleans. General Houston had now been nearly forty days without medicine or poultices; the bandages for his wound he had torn from the shirt he wore, till all but its bosom was gone—for he had given all he had away to the soldiers as their necessities had before been greater than his own. He was now, as he supposed, in a dying state. He was so feeble, he could not even be raised up without fainting. In passing the English Turn, about eighteen miles below New Orleans, it was known by expresses in waiting that Houston was on board, and it was the first confirmation of the news of the battle. It was Sunday, and the levee was black with the dense crowd which, as the intelligence spread through the city, had rushed together to see the wounded soldier. His friend, Colonel Christy, with whom he had served as lieutenant in his youth, had prepared for him in his house every comfort his situation required, and he was now eager to grasp the hand of his old comrade, and extend him the most cordial welcome. Dr. Kerr, too, who had operated on his wounds just thirty years before, hastened to the vessel, where he found him lying on the deck. He fell upon him, and embraced him like a father. He, with Dr. Cenas, gave him every attention, and they saved his life; for they said if he had arrived a few hours later, he could not have been saved, since his wound had begun to show the first symptoms of mortification. The crowd on the boat was so great, it was in danger of sinking, and the throng so dense on the pier, it was a long time before he could be got ashore. An unsuccessful attempt had been made to lift him ashore, but it seemed he would die of torture before it could be done. At last, feeling that his strength was going, he rose on his crutches, and, by a desperate effort, got over the gunwale himself. He was immediately laid upon a litter, where he fainted again.

In the meantime, bands of music had come down to the pier, and were playing martial airs, while the landing was being effected. The cot, which had been prepared, was brought up, and Houston, who seemed to be dying, was borne through the vast throng to the hospitable mansion of his friend, where this skeleton of disease and suffering at last found repose.

He remained about two weeks in New Orleans, and although he was far from being out of danger, yet his anxiety to return to Texas was so great, that he took passage to Natchitoches, on the Red River. The fatigue and exposure of the journey were too much for his feeble health, and he was obliged to stop several days to recover his strength. But the first moment he was able, he traveled on to San Augustine, where he remained till the news came that the cabinet had made a treaty with Santa Anna, and were resolved on his liberation. At the same time it was stated that the enemy was preparing for another campaign. Demonstrations of respect had been made, and dinners offered to him at New Orleans, Natchitoches, and San Augustine; but he declined all such compliments. The report of the advance of the enemy had brought together a vast concourse of people at San Augustine. Houston was taken to the meeting, and, resting on his crutches, delivered an address, which produced such an effect, that one hundred and sixty men in two days, took up their march for the frontier.

Soon after, the general received intelligence that Colonels Millard and Wheelock had been dispatched from the army then at the Coleto, with a demand on the cabinet that they should deliver up Santa Anna into their hands for execution, reproaching them for the neglect of their duty, and an order to arrest President Burnet, and bring him to the Texian camp. Houston immediately dispatched the following protest against their proceedings, by express to the army.

Ayish Bayou, 26th July, 1836.
To The General Commanding the Army of Texas.

Sir—I have just heard through a citizen, of the army, that it is the intention to remove General Santa Anna to the army, and place him upon his trial. I cannot credit this statement; it is obviously contrary to the true policy of Texas. The advantages which his capture presented to us will be destroyed. Disregard, if you will, our national character, and place what construction you please upon the rules of civilized warfare, we are compelled by every principle of humanity and morality, to abstain from every act of passion or inconsideration that is to be unproductive of positive good. Execute Santa Anna, and what will be the fate of the Texians who are held prisoners by the Mexicans—what will be the condition of the North Americans who are residing within the limits of Mexico? Death to them, and confiscation of their property is the least that can be expected. Doubtless torture will be added to the catastrophe, when stimulated by ignorance, fanaticism, and the last expiring struggle of the priesthood for power and dominion. Texas, to be respected, must be considerate, politic and just in her actions. Santa Anna, living and secured beyond all danger of escape, in the eastern section of Texas (as I first suggested), may be of incalculable advantage to Texas in her present crisis. In cool blood to offer up the living to the manes of the departed, only finds an example in the religion and warfare of savages. Regard for one's departed friends should stimulate us in the hour of battle, and would excuse us in the moment of victory, for partial excesses, at which our calmer feelings of humanity would relent.

The affairs of Texas connected with General Santa Anna, as President of the Republic of Mexico, have become matter of consideration to which the attention of the United States has been called, and for Texas, at this moment, to proceed to extreme measures, as to the merits or demerits of General Santa Anna, would be treating that Government with high disrespect, and I would respectfully add, in my opinion, it would be incurring the most unfortunate responsibility for Texas.

I, therefore, Commander-in-Chief of the army of the Republic, do solemnly protest against the trial, sentence, and execution of General Antonio Lopez de Santa Anna, President of the Republic of Mexico, until the relations in which we are to stand to the United States shall be ascertained.

SAM HOUSTON,
COMMANDER-IN-CHIEF OF THE ARMY.

This protest had just the effect designed by the writer. The trial of Santa Anna was delayed, and Texas was saved from the disgrace and execration which so summary and barbarous a proceeding would have brought upon her name. Soon after this, Houston removed to Nacogdoches, where he remained under the influence of his wound till fall. But he was far from being idle, for the country was under a quasi state of martial law, and the exigency called for his constant vigilance and advice.

In the meantime we must glance rapidly over the events which were elsewhere taking place. The cabinet perceiving that Houston's views, officially communicated to General Rusk, were founded upon the highest principles of policy, humanity, and justice, adopted them in the main in the treaty they made with Santa Anna, on the 14th of May. The President and his cabinet were still at Velasco on the first of June, and the Texian schooner *Invincible* was anchored off the bar, in sight of the town, with Santa Anna and his suite on board, and the sailing orders of the vessel had been issued for her to proceed to Vera Cruz. Santa Anna wrote the following FAREWELL

TO THE TEXIAN ARMY:

> My friends! I have been a witness of your courage in the field
> of battle, and know you to be generous. Rely with confidence
> on my sincerity, and you shall never have cause to regret the
> kindness shown me. In returning to my native land, I beg you
> to receive the sincere thanks of your grateful friend. Farewell.
>
> ANT. LOPEZ DE SANTA ANNA.
> *Velasco, 1st June, 1836.*

I know not what may be the opinions of others, but I am persuaded that Santa Anna never would have committed himself
in *this* manner, when there was no necessity of doing it (for it
was written *after* the vessel was under sailing orders), unless he
really intended to redeem his pledge. For although he had entered into a solemn treaty, yet his own conscience and the whole
world would have palliated any violation of that treaty (which
was wrung from him by his captors; for what will not a prisoner
promise to buy his liberty? they would have said), much sooner
than they would have forgiven the violation of private pledges,
voluntarily given by a *free* man. No such pledges were now necessary; he was perfectly free to give or withhold them. Any bad
faith subsequently manifested, would have been regarded as the
blackest perfidy, and Texas would have gained more, perhaps
(if she had kept *her* faith inviolate) by his treachery, than she
would have lost; for her honor and her magnanimity, and the
perfidy of Santa Anna, would have won for her the sympathy
of the civilized world! But an event now took place which I
must regard as a public and a lasting calamity to Texas.

General Green arrived at Velasco, with several hundred volunteers from the United States, just as the *Invincible* was sailing.
This individual, who had not, as yet, participated in the Texian
struggle, and who, in fact, had yet no authority to order a drum
beat in Texas, set himself at once in opposition to the government, and declared that the *Invincible* should not be allowed to
lift her anchor. He was determined Santa Anna should be tried

and executed! It is unnecessary to indulge in any exclamations of censure for this high-handed abuse of military power. Popular feeling was on his side, and Mr. Lamar had already protested (in a voluminous paper) against Santa Anna's release. The president *ad interim* at last yielded to this outrageous violation of the public faith, and although the treaty had been signed, sealed, and delivered, and Santa Anna had it with him on board, and the vessel was under sailing orders, yet he countermanded her orders, and sent a requisition on board for the Mexican president.

Santa Anna was aware what had been the popular feeling towards him from the day of his capture; and he undoubtedly believed that his life would be in danger in the hands of a president who would violate a solemn treaty. Under such circumstances he resolutely refused to go on shore. The order was repeated the next day, and it provoked a similar reply. On the afternoon of the third of June, General Green, with several armed men, "visited the *Invincible*" (says Foote, 2 vol., p. 342), "for the purpose of bringing off the dictator, dead or alive." Santa Anna remonstrated against the lawless outrage, and, like a brave man, declared he would die before he left. "All this time," says General Green (p. 343), "he lay on his back in his berth, and his respiration seemed to be exceedingly difficult." No wonder such a display of the boasted Anglo-Saxon faith should disturb the respiration even of a Mexican! All other means failing, General Green ordered him to be *put in irons*. "When the irons were brought within his view, the prisoner immediately jumped up, adjusted his collar, put on his hat, and stated his readiness to accompany us" (p. 343). And how else would you have a defenseless prisoner act, with a score of bayonets or bowie-knives at his breast? For my own part, I know of no circumstance in Santa Anna's history so worthy of admiration as his conduct on this occasion; nor do I know of any act of perfidy or cowardice equal to that evinced by his lawless aggressors.

I am no eulogist of Santa Anna. I consider him an ambitious, selfish, military chieftain, who has trampled on the constitution, and blotted out the liberties of his country. But to his honor be it said, that he was not the first to violate the treaty of the 14th of May. Like a brave man, too, he boldly protested against the perfidy of the Texian cabinet.

He said: "I had embarked on the Texian schooner-of-war, the *Invincible*, on the 1st of June, after addressing a short farewell to the Texians, wherein I thanked them for their generous behavior, and offered my eternal gratitude. And I protest... for the act of violence committed on my person, and abuse to which I have been exposed, in being compelled to go on shore, merely because 130 volunteers, under the command of Gen. Thos. Green, recently landed on the beach at Velasco, from New Orleans, had with tumults and threats demanded that my person should be placed at their disposal, which took place on the very day the government received from Gen. Filisola the answer that he had strictly fulfilled what had been stipulated in the treaty. * * Under these circumstances, I appeal to the judgment of civilized nations, to the consciences of the citizens who compose the Cabinet, and, above all, to the Supreme Ruler of the destinies of nations, who has placed the existence and happiness of nations on the faith of treaties and punctual fulfillment of engagements."

If I am pointed to Goliad and the Alamo, my only reply is, that such an appeal to the civilized world and to the Supreme Ruler of nations from the perpetrator of those massacres, only makes his sarcasm on Texian faith the more bitter.

And yet all the blame of this infamous proceeding belongs to a military adventurer, the gratification of whose love of notoriety was dearer than the faith of a government plighted to a prisoner. If it be said that the president *ad interim* was *obliged* to yield to the clamor of the populace, who were thirsting for Santa Anna's blood, I reply that he could not have been *compelled*, by any mortal power, to write with his own hand the requisition for Santa Anna—had he been a man of nerve enough to fit him to hold the reins of power in revolutionary times. When Houston was asked what he would have done in the same circumstances, he said, "I would have regarded the faith of the nation under any circumstances, and before the mob should have laid hands on Santa Anna, they should have first drunk my blood." It now became perfectly certain that all the hopes of advantage Houston had borrowed from the treaty and the release of Santa Anna, were to be disappointed. He knew that the only reliance they had or could have was upon his gratitude and sense of honor, and now the course his enemies had taken had dissolved all his obligations.

After Mr. Lamar resigned his post as Secretary of War, the cabinet appointed him commander-in-chief of the army, over the heads of Generals Houston and Rusk. He immediately repaired to the army with his commission, and surrounded by his staff. The army was drawn up; after addressing them, he requested an expression of their sentiments. They were anxious for Houston again to assume the command, and in the meantime were perfectly satisfied with Gen. Rusk. But Mr. Lamar wished some more decided demonstration, and they were ordered, by marching in different directions, to indicate their feelings towards the new commander. There were about 1,800 troops in the camp—less than one in eighteen voted for him, and the rest positively refused to serve under him! He thus acquired the title of General, and got rid of the responsibilities of command.

CHAPTER X:
THE PRESIDENT

The government *ad interim* at last became disgusted with power. The people felt that when Houston was away they had no one to repose on, and discontent became universal. Provision had been made by the Convention for the crisis, and writs were issued for the election of a President by the people of Texas.

There were two candidates—Gen. Stephen F. Austin, and Ex-Governor Henry Smith. They were both excellent men, particularly Gen. Austin, whom we have had occasion so often to mention with respect. Houston had been importuned from the beginning to become a candidate, but he had refused, nor did he consent till twelve days before the election. He wished to retire from public life, for he believed there would be no necessity of firing another hostile gun in Texas if the public councils were guided by firmness and wisdom. He had been unrelentingly persecuted, and his feelings outraged, just in proportion as he had devoted himself to the State. In retirement, he could be happy, and his country free. He was, therefore, disinclined to mingle in the turmoil of public life. But one motive at last overcame his objections.

He believed (such was the virulence of party) that if either of the candidates should succeed, their cabinets would be made up exclusively of party men, which would endanger the stability of the administration. A government was to be created from chaos, without a dollar and without credit. The parties were pretty equally balanced, and there was great reason to fear that those out of power would so far embarrass the administration as to destroy its efficiency. He believed, that since he belonged to neither party, and possessed the confidence of the great mass of the people, he might still render signal service to the state, and he allowed his name to be used.

At the announcement, the turbulence of party everywhere gave way to a national enthusiasm. None but his enemies thought of opposing his election, and they were only a feeble clique of adventurers, who had rushed to Texas when her agitations began, hoping to win, in the turbulent scenes of Revolution, a notoriety they had in vain sought for in the calmer scenes of civic life. The provisional government of '35, and the administration of '36, had proved they were incapable of holding the reins of government over a frontier population. The people at last saw that they must place some man at the helm whose strong hand would steady the vessel through the boisterous surges. They knew there was but one man in Texas who could sway the multitude, and when the hero of San Jacinto consented to accept the presidency, they offered it to him by acclamation.

Houston had indeed displayed those rare qualities which make the great general. It now remained to be seen if he was endowed with those loftier and nobler qualities, which would fit him for the cabinet—for a far more difficult task now remained, in the organization of a government which should secure peace, and power, and prosperity at home, and command the respect of civilized nations—than it had been to win even the brilliant victory of San Jacinto. Senators and representatives were elected at the same time, and on the 3rd of October (1836), the delegates assembled at Columbia, and the first Congress of the Republic of Texas was organized.

On the morning of the 22nd of the same month, the president *ad interim* tendered his resignation, and a resolution was immediately introduced, "that the inauguration take place at four o'clock this day." A committee from both Houses waited upon the President-elect, and at four o'clock, he was introduced within the bar of the House of Representatives. The Speaker administered to him the oath of office, and then proclaimed Sam Houston President of the Republic of Texas. Advancing to the table, he delivered an extemporaneous inaugural address. We consider it important the reader should be furnished with it entire, for it unfolds the policy of Houston's administration, and it could never have been spoken but by a great statesman. It will be consulted by future times as the most important State paper that will be found in the early archives of Texas. We give it as it came from the reporter of the Congress.

Mr. Speaker and Gentlemen:

Deeply impressed with a sense of the responsibility devolving on me, I cannot, in justice to myself, repress the emotion of my heart, or restrain the feelings which my sense of obligation to my fellow citizens has inspired—their suffrage was gratuitously bestowed. Preferred to others, not unlikely superior in merit to myself, called to the most important station among mankind, by the voice of a free people, it is utterly impossible not to feel impressed with the deepest sensations of delicacy, in my present position before the world. It is not here alone, but our present attitude before all nations, has rendered my position, and that of my country, one of peculiar interest.

A spot of earth almost unknown to the geography of the age, destitute of all available resources, few in numbers, we remonstrated against oppression; and when invaded by a numerous host, we dared to proclaim our Independence and to strike for freedom on the breast of the oppressor. As yet our course is onward. We are only in the outset of the campaign of liberty. Futurity has locked up the destiny which awaits our people. Who can contemplate with apathy a situation so imposing in the moral and physical world! No one. The relations among ourselves are peculiarly delicate and important; for no matter what zeal or fidelity I may possess in the discharge of my official duties, if I do not obtain cooperation and an honest support from the coordinate departments of the government, wreck and ruin must be the inevitable consequences of my administration. If then, in the discharge of my duty, my competency should fail in the attainment of the great objects in view, it would become your sacred duty to correct my errors and sustain me by your superior wisdom. This much I anticipate—this much I demand.

I am perfectly aware of the difficulties that surround me, and the convulsive throes through which our country must pass. I have never been emulous of the civic wreath—when merited it crowns a happy destiny. A country situated like ours, is environed with difficulties, its administration is fraught with perplexities. Had it been my destiny I would infinitely have preferred the toils, privations, and perils of a soldier, to the duties of my present station. Nothing but zeal, stimulated by the holy spirit of patriotism, and guided by philosophy and reason, can give that impetus to our energies necessary to surmount the difficulties that obstruct our political progress. By the aid of your intelligence, I trust all impediments in our advancement will be removed; that all wounds in the body politic will be healed, and the Constitution of the Republic derive strength and vigor equal to any emergency. I shall confidently anticipate the establishment of Constitutional liberty. In the attainment of this object, we must regard our relative situation to other countries.

A subject of no small importance is the situation of an extensive frontier, bordered by Indians, and open to their depredation. Treaties of peace and amity and the maintenance of good faith with the Indians, seem to me the most rational means for winning their friendship. Let us abstain from aggression, establish commerce with the different tribes, supply their useful and necessary wants, maintain even-handed justice with them, and natural reason will teach them the utility of our friendship.

Admonished by the past, we cannot, in justice, disregard our national enemies. Vigilance will apprise us of their approach, a disciplined and valiant army will insure their discomfiture. Without discrimination and system, how unavailing would all the resources of an old and overflowing treasury prove to us. It would be as unprofitable to us in our present situation, as the rich diamond locked in the bosom of the adamant. We cannot hope that the bosom of our beautiful prairies will soon be visited by the healing breezes of peace. We may again look for the day when their verdure will be converted into dyes of crimson. We must keep all our energies alive, our army organized, disciplined, and increased to our present emergencies. With these preparations we can meet and vanquish despotic thousands. This is the attitude we at present must regard as our own. We are battling for human liberty; reason and firmness must characterize our acts.

The course our enemies have pursued has been opposed to every principle of civilized warfare—bad faith, inhumanity and devastation, marked their path of invasion. We were a little band, contending for liberty—they were thousands, well appointed, munitioned and provisioned, seeking to rivet chains upon us, or extirpate us from the earth. Their cruelties have incurred the universal denunciation of Christendom. They will not pass from their nation during the present generation. The contrast of our conduct is manifest; we were hunted down as the felon wolf, our little band driven from fastness to fastness, exasperated to the last extreme; while the blood of our kindred and our friends invoking the vengeance of an offended God was smoking to high heaven, we met our enemy and vanquished them. They fell in battle, or suppliantly kneeled and were spared. We offered up our vengeance at the shrine of humanity, while Christianity rejoiced at the act and looked with pride on the sacrifice. The civilized world contemplated with proud emotions, conduct which reflected so much glory on the Anglo-Saxon race. The moral effect has done more towards our liberation, than the defeat of the army of veterans. Where our cause has been presented to our friends in the land of our origin, they have embraced it with their warmest sympathies. They have rendered us manly and efficient aids. They have rallied to our standard, they have fought side by side with our warriors. They have bled, and their dust is mingling with the ashes of our heroes. At this moment I discern numbers around me, who battled in the field of San Jacinto, and whose chivalry and valor have identified them with the glory of the country, its name, its soil, and its liberty. There sits a gentleman within my view, whose personal and political services to Texas have been invaluable. He was the first in the United States to respond to our cause. His purse was ever open to our necessities. His hand was extended in our aid. His presence among us and his return to the embraces of our friends will inspire new efforts in behalf of our cause. The attention of the Speaker and that of Congress, was directed to Wm. Christy, Esq., of New Orleans, who sat by invitation within the bar. A circumstance of the highest import will claim the attention of the court at Washington. In our recent election, the important subject of annexation to the United States of America was submitted to the consideration of the people. They have expressed their feelings and their wishes on that momentous subject. They have, with a unanimity unparalleled, declared that they will be reunited to the Great Republican family of the North. The appeal is made by a willing people. Will our friends disregard it? They have already bestowed upon us their warmest sympathies. Their manly and generous feelings have been enlisted on our behalf. We are cheered by the hope that they will receive us to participate in their civil, political, and religious rights, and hail us welcome into the great family of freemen. Our misfortunes have been their misfortunes—our sorrows, too, have been theirs, and their joy at our success has been irrepressible.

A thousand considerations press upon me, each claims my attention. But the shortness of the notice of this emergency (for the Speaker had only four hours' notice of the inauguration, and all this time was spent in conversation) will not enable me to do justice to those subjects, and will necessarily induce their postponement for the present. [Here the President, says the reporter, paused for a few seconds and disengaged his sword.] It now, sir, becomes my duty to make a presentation of this sword—this emblem of my past office. [The President was unable to proceed further; but having firmly clenched it with both hands, as if with a farewell grasp, a tide of varied associations rushed upon him in the moment, his countenance bespoke the workings of the strongest emotions, his soul seemed to dwell momentarily on the glistening blade, and the greater part of the auditory gave outward proof of their congeniality of feeling. It was in reality a moment of deep and painful interest. After this pause, more eloquently impressive than the deepest pathos conveyed in language, the President proceeded.] I have worn it with some humble pretensions in defense of my country,—and should the danger of my country again call for my services, I expect to resume it, and respond to that call, if needful, with my blood and my life.

The first step the president took in his administration; evinced his political forecast and the broad national principles on which he intended to govern the country. He chose his two most important cabinet officers from his rivals for the presidency; General Austin, the incorruptible patriot, became Secretary of State, and Ex-Provisional Governor Henry Smith, Secretary of the Treasury. This selection was not only magnanimous, but it was high policy. The rancor of party subsided—the oil calmed the turbid waters. It evinced the important fact, that Houston had no party but country, and no aim but the public good.

Everything was in chaos. The archives of the State were hurled loosely together in an old trunk—everything had to be done. Although the cabinet was composed of apparently so discordant materials, yet all their proceedings were characterized by harmony, till Mr. Austin's death, which took place in a few months. He was deeply regretted by his people, for he was an upright, enlightened and purely patriotic man. Congress was now completely organized, and public business was being done in an orderly and efficient manner.

When Houston arrived at Columbia, for the inauguration, he found that his former captive, Santa Anna, was still retained a prisoner about twelve miles from the seat of government, under a guard of twenty men. Santa Anna sent word to Houston, that he would be very glad if he could have the pleasure of seeing him. He did not send to implore his release—for he seems to have given up nearly all hope of ever regaining his liberty. But in Houston he had found a magnanimous foe, and he wished to see his conqueror.

The reader can readily imagine how Houston was affected by such a message from a prisoner, to whose release the government *ad interim* had pledged its most solemn faith, and then left him to drag out months of weary imprisonment. He still felt as he had in the beginning, and he determined to wipe out the stain of dishonor from the name of Texas. "After a victory—like San Jacinto," said he, "we could richly have afforded to have been *magnanimous*—now the only question is, can we afford to be just?" He knew, besides, there were no means in the government to support captives. It had been in a state of quasi dissolution for months. Santa Anna and his friends had been living on a mere pittance, destitute of the comforts and many of the necessaries of life. Houston took with him several gentlemen and went to visit the prisoner. Those who were present have represented their meeting as rather affecting. Santa Anna, after the custom of his nation, opened his arms and came forward to meet his visitor. Houston, whose great heart was large enough to hold even his enemies, received him in like manner, and as the worn captive rested his head on Houston's broad breast (for he hardly came up to his shoulder), they say that the two generals wept together—the Mexican at the recollection of his reverses—the Virginian sympathizing with the man he had vanquished.

Through Almonte, who still acted as their interpreter, and in the presence of Patton and others, Santa Anna appealed to his conqueror to interpose his power in his behalf, and adverted to the letter he had himself written to Gen. Jackson, and enclosed to Houston at Nacogdoches. Jackson had answered his letter in very kind terms, and passed a high eulogium upon his friend Gen. Houston, for his magnanimity towards his captive. Indeed, Gen. Jackson often declared that Houston deserved and would receive as much honor from all great and good men for his treatment of Santa Anna after the victory, as for the victory itself. "Let those who clamor for blood," said the brave old hero, "clamor on. The world will take care of Houston's fame."

Houston was not yet inaugurated, but he assured the Mexican general that he would remember him. Col. Christy (who bore Texas on his heart, and was jealous of her honor) and other generous men, had sent some comforts to Santa Anna a short time before, and Houston and some of his friends dined with him that day, and then they parted. Santa Anna wrote Houston after his return to Columbia. The communication was laid before Congress, and his release solicited. The matter was referred to committees of both houses, and a report was made of a most inflammatory character. In a secret session the Senate passed a resolution requiring his detention as a prisoner. Houston responded in a calm, dignified veto, showing the impolicy of a longer detention—the probability of his being assassinated (as one attempt had already been made before Houston's arrival), and whether he might die from violence or disease, that Texas never would escape the odium of his death. The Senate reversed their decision, and referred the matter to the discretion of the President. He expressed the belief that if Santa Anna was restored to his country, he would keep Mexico in commotion for years and Texas would be safe.

Houston determined at once to release him on his own responsibility. He informed him that if he wished to visit Washington, as Gen. Jackson had requested, he should have an escort, chosen by himself. Santa Anna returned his thanks by the messenger, and requested that Cols. Hockley and Bee, and Major Patton be allowed to attend him. About the 25th of November, the escort departed, and Houston went with them to take his final leave of the liberated captive. The parting took place and the little party set out on fine horses, for the Sabine. They lost their way in the prairie, and it so happened that they were compelled, in regaining it, to pass over the battleground of San Jacinto! When Santa Anna saw the bones of his soldiers whitening on the field, he was deeply affected, and the gentlemanly men who attended him, seeming not to observe his agitation, rode leisurely on and left the deserted general to indulge his feelings on the field of his slain.

Santa Anna is a great man. He has a Mexican education and Mexican principles, but an American intellect of high order. He is a great general. He has a fine face—a rather long, but well-shaped head—black hair and eyes, and a *perfect form*—he is about five feet and seven or nine inches high—his elocution is rich, and characterized by considerable fire—his eye is quick, but firm, and his manners and address are worthy of a prince.

In the beginning of his administration the President appointed Colonel William H. Wharton, Minister to Washington, with instructions to commence negotiations with General Jackson for the annexation of Texas to the United States. Soon after Memucan Hunt, Esq., was appointed to act in concert with him. During the summer of 1836, General Jackson had dispatched a confidential agent to Texas. He explored its territory, scrutinized its government, mingled in its society, made himself familiar with its resources, and reported fully to the President. His report satisfied the President and his cabinet that Texas was entitled, by the Law of Nations, to a recognition of her independence, and although his own sympathies were with that people in their struggle, and from the hour they achieved their independence he never had a doubt they would one day be annexed to the United States, yet he wisely withheld the expression of such an opinion, and did not even press upon Congress the recognition.

In his message of the 5th of December, 1836, after assigning the most satisfactory reasons, he says, "Our character requires that we should neither anticipate events, nor attempt to control them." And alluding to the desire of Texas for annexation, he says: "Necessarily a work of time, and uncertain in itself, it is calculated to expose our conduct to misconstruction in the eyes of the world." On the twenty-second of the same month, the President, in another message, after discussing the question, expresses his opinion that it would be impolitic yet to recognize Texas as an independent state, and then proposes to acquiesce in the decision of Congress. The question was not brought up again till the 12th of January, 1837, when Mr. Walker, Senator from Mississippi, introduced the following resolution:

> *Resolved,* That the State of Texas having established and maintained an independent Government, is capable of performing those duties, foreign and domestic, which appertain to Independent Governments; and it appearing that there is no longer any reasonable prospect of the successful prosecution of the war by Mexico against said State, it is expedient and proper, and in conformity with the Laws of Nations, and the practice of this Government in like cases, that the independent political existence of that State be acknowledged by the Government of the United States.

The Senate was not prepared for immediate action on the question, and Mr. Walker knew it. He was aware that the strange and disgraceful war which the American press had so generally begun to wage against the interests and advancement of Texian liberty, had colored the prejudices, and would control the votes of senators, and he determined to bide his time. Mr. Walker moved that his resolution be made the order of the day for the 18th of January; but when the time came it was crowded aside. Several ineffectual attempts were made to decide the question, and at last it was brought up on the 1st of March for final action. An able and brilliant debate followed; Messrs. Preston, Crittenden, Clay, and Calhoun, all sustained the Mississippi Senator with the persuasive power of their eloquence. Mr. Clay spoke of Texas with generous enthusiasm, and unhesitatingly declared that her Constitution, as a whole, was superior to that of the United States. How different might have been the political fortunes of that truly great and patriotic man, and the fortunes of his party, if he had, to the end, pursued the same high and sagacious policy towards that beautiful country! But his course, as well as Mr. Van Buren's, only furnishes us with another impressive illustration how few great men, even, are able to withstand the clamor of party in turbulent times.

The measure prevailed by a small majority. For the success of the measure Texas was indebted to the efforts of Mr. Walker, and his course in the affair entitled him to the regards of the entire nation. The day will come, too, when the mists that have obscured the gaze of the people and their statesmen shall have cleared away, and the name of the Mississippi Senator will everywhere be mentioned with honor and with gratitude. Texas will build his monument, and give it a conspicuous place in the temple she will erect for those who proved themselves her friends in the day of trial. The grateful Republic commissioned the portrait of Mr. Preston, and the bust of Mr. Walker, for her Capitol. The last time General Jackson ever put his pen officially to paper, was to sign the resolution recognizing Texas an independent state. Such was the earliest fruit of the mission of those intelligent and accomplished men whom General Houston commissioned to the court of Washington. We have read their correspondence with the two governments, and we have seldom perused abler state papers.

In March, 1837, the seat of government was removed from Columbia on the Brazos, to Houston, which stands on the highest point of navigation on the bayou that empties into Galveston Bay. There was but one house in Houston. It was a cabin just erected, and in it the president of the new nation took up his abode. His floor was the ground, where the grass was growing. But population rushed in, and in a short time comfortable public buildings were erected.

Houston's policy in regard to the future was to obtain annexation if possible. If this could not be done, he was determined to conduct the government on principles that would secure confidence abroad and inspire hope at home. The proposition for annexation had been rejected by our government, and such was the state of feeling at the time in the United States, Houston had no expectation of the early success of that grand measure, in whose consummation the keen-sighted statesmen of both countries saw so many elements of mutual power and prosperity. He was therefore determined to lay the foundations of the Texian Republic deep and strong—to husband its resources—never to cripple the state with a public debt—to harmonize warring factions—to be the ruler of the Nation, and not of a party or a *clique*.

The cultivation of friendly relations with the powerful and warlike savage tribes on the frontier, he regarded as one of the most important objects of his administration. This ferocious population not only outnumbered all the inhabitants of Texas, but they could not be conquered. The Comanches, the most numerous and savage tribe, live in the saddle. They can move with their women and children with great celerity whenever and wherever their necessities or their passions carry them; they can make their incursions without the possibility of pursuit from their enemies. They are hordes of barbarians, as ferocious as Cossacks and as fleet as the Bedouins of the desert. And yet, such was Houston's knowledge of the Indian character, and so rigidly did he regard the letter and spirit of his treaties with those fearful tribes, he saved the Republic from their incursions and made them venerate and love his name.

In a former part of this work, we have given the views of Houston on the subject of our treatment of the Indians. Those views have been regarded by many as utterly chimerical; and yet if we had space we could show that during his two administrations in Texas, he carried them out successfully; and he has often declared that, in no instance where he had an opportunity of giving the Indians evidence that he intended to treat them with good faith and with common justice, did he experience the slightest difficulty in winning their friendship and preserving their perpetual alliance. In all these negotiations the great secret of his power over those wily red men, consisted in two things. His associations with the Indians gave him a complete knowledge of their character—and he treated with them on the great principles of humanity and justice.

And yet the government was destitute of all the ordinary means of support. They had not a dollar, nor could loans be obtained. An army was in the field, but they could not be supported. When Congress met at Houston, General Felix Huston, who commanded the army, hurried to the place. He had projected a grand campaign against Matamoros. Every man who felt jealous of the influence of the president joined in the scheme. The army now numbered over 2,400 men. The president foresaw the consequences of these movements.

There was no money in the treasury, or means, or currency, except promissory notes, struck on common paper. It was clearly impossible to conduct a campaign. The president saw what the upshot of this matter would be if something were not done at once, and he resorted to a sagacious expedient. Col. Rodgers, now left in command of the army, had caused it to be understood that, if the volunteers did not get justice, he would march with them to the seat of government, "chastise the President, kick Congress out of doors, and give laws to Texas."

At this crisis the president determined to cut the evil up by the roots. General Felix Huston had occasionally indulged his men in what he called a *Saturnalia*, where murders had occurred in consequence of the brutal intoxication of the men. One evening, from intelligence of what was doing in Congress (for he never visited the House, except at the opening or close of the Session), Houston directed the Secretary of War to be ready to start the next morning, at two o'clock, for the camp. He handed him sealed orders, to be opened in the camp, and ordered him to go there with all possible dispatch. These orders required the Secretary to furlough the army by companies, until they were reduced to six hundred men. The first company was furloughed to march to Dimitt's Landing, on Matagorda Bay; the second to the mouth of the Brazos; the third to Galveston; and this process was continued till the reduction was made.

His object was to give them an opportunity to get to the United States by water, and thus relieve the country from apprehensions. The furloughs given to the men were unlimited, but they were liable to be recalled at any time by proclamation; and if they did not report themselves in thirty days after the proclamation they were to be considered deserters, and treated as such. Houston could not disband the army, for there was nothing to pay them off with; and he had been taught a lesson by the attempt of General Washington to disband the army of the North. And yet, so entirely had all subordination been broken down—daring scenes of violence were so constantly occurring at the camp—so many lawless and desperate men were banded together, to commit high-handed depredations—that the whole country began to suffer the most serious apprehensions. Houston manifested no alarm, but the course he took bespoke his fears. He was determined that the army should be disbanded, and he accomplished his purpose in his own way.

When the various companies reached their destinations, no longer held together by the bond which union had before given, they thought they had seen enough of military life. They had fared roughly; and their surplus chivalry had so completely oozed out of the holes in their coats, that they no longer had courage enough to be dangerous; and—fearing they would not get out of the country before the proclamation was issued—they made the best of their way to the United States. In thirty days they had all disappeared; and when the *finale* was known throughout the country, every man felt that Houston had saved the nation from the deepest peril. It was, in fact, a stroke of bold, but sagacious policy, which none but a man like him would have dared to attempt. General Felix Huston was plotting at the capital but before he knew what the president was doing, his army was disbanded.

About this time a Land Law was passed, under which all the troubles about *titles* have grown up. Its object was speculation, and many voted for it anticipating enormous gains. Houston vetoed it in one of his ablest state papers. But his veto was not supported, and the law went into operation. A few years showed its malign and fatal fruits. It opened the door to all sorts of fraud, and was a fruitful source of lasting litigation. This was but a single specimen of the recklessness of legislation in the Congress of Texas. (During Houston's two terms he issued not less than eighty vetoes.) Had there not been a firm and intelligent statesman at the head of the government, no man can tell where such Congresses would have plunged the nation.

Another law was passed, authorizing an excessive issue of promissory notes. This also the president vetoed, and he declared that if the measure prevailed the paper would soon depreciate ten to one. He arrested this fatal proceeding for a time. It passed under the administration of his successor, and his prophecy was abundantly fulfilled.

During the year 1837 the country was agitated by occasional alarms of Mexican and Indian invasions, but Houston was on the alert, and nothing of the kind took place. The utmost confidence in his administration prevailed among the people; and the beautiful spectacle was presented of an industrious and increasing population, which had just recovered from the shock and the devastation of a powerful invading army, and environed with Mexican and savage foes, quietly and successfully prosecuting the arts of peace. Houston proclaimed trade and intercourse between Mexico and Texas, and caused his proclamation to be printed and circulated in both languages. Trade grew up rapidly; the frontier counties were repopulated; and the tide of emigration was gradually flowing towards the Mexican borders. Caravans of horses and mules came into Texas, with large quantities of silver and merchandise; good feeling was fast growing up, and continued to increase. Men, on both sides of the line, were now anxious for peace. The Mexican people had nothing to gain in battle, and had the renewal of hostilities depended on the vote of the Mexican population, both countries would have been blessed with lasting peace.

We must now close our brief account of Houston's first administration. The proposition for annexation had been steadily pressed upon the attention of the government at Washington. But the Texian ministers received little encouragement, and as Texas could promise herself no advantage from farther negotiations, Houston withdrew the proposition. He believed that any further attempts to consummate that great measure would prejudice Texas in the eyes of other nations; and in withdrawing the proposal his conduct met the approval of the nation. His presidential term closed the 12th of December, 1838. He went out of office, leaving a government perfectly organized; with officers of ability, integrity, and economy in every department of the State. The nation was not more than a million and a half in debt, with about $600,000 of promissory notes in circulation. Texas had peace with the Indians and commerce with Mexico. The feuds between the two nations were dying away, and the promissory notes were at par. This circumstance is, perhaps, the clearest and most convincing proof of the great ability and integrity with which Houston had conducted the government. There was little specie in the country—how these notes were ever to be redeemed the people did not know—but they said, "As long as Old Sam is at the helm the ship is safe." They were voyaging through stormy seas, but they knew they were sailing with Caesar.

No man was ever confronted with greater difficulties in the beginning of his administration—for the mild but firm sway of constitutional law had to be substituted in the place of anarchy and confusion, over a reckless people who had long been accustomed to the unrestrained liberty of the frontier, where no man looked for protection but in his own right arm. During these revolutionary times, too, even in the older settlements, the ordinary course of justice had been suspended, and it was no strange thing that such men should not at once yield to the high supremacy of constitutional law.

The very same elements of character, which have long made the Anglo-Saxons the most law-abiding people on the globe, have always made them the most lawless frontiermen. Men who choose their homes in the distant forest or prairie, are slow to transfer their protection from their rifles, which never miss fire, to tardy juries which seldom mete out justice. How long was it before that wonderful people, that first scared the wild beasts from the solemn forests of the Tiber, voted to abide by the awards of the Temple of Justice! And how many centuries did our ancestors roam over the beautiful Island of Britain, dressed in the skins of wild beasts, before they would listen to the stern utterances of judicial tribunals. But Houston could sway those reckless frontier settlers by the mild scepter of civil law as easily as he had swayed them by the stern despotism of the camp.

But while he was successfully accomplishing these benign changes, and rearing the noble structure of civil government, he was not only harassed by petty intrigues, but confronted with formidable combinations. The same clique of small but ambitious men, who had from the beginning busied themselves in inventing means to undermine the castle which they could not overthrow, while Houston was bleeding on the field, or toiling anxiously in the cabinet, finding all their intrigues fruitless, at last cemented themselves as well as they could, into one organized conspiracy, bent upon his destruction. Their history would be a story of all that is exciting in faction and mean in selfishness. But we have neither time nor inclination to chronicle their doings—nor would we snatch them from the oblivion to which they seem to be hastening.

Houston's conduct throughout the country met with the warmest approval, and he would have been the almost unanimous choice of the people, had he been eligible to the office, the next term. But the 2nd Section of the Third Article of the Constitution declared that, "The First President elected by the people shall hold his office for the term of two years, and shall be ineligible during the next succeeding term." An accident gave the presidency to Mr. Lamar. Just before the election his rival died!—and no other candidate was brought forward.

It had been said that the president-elect would be the idol of the State, and that Houston's power was gone. The hour of his resignation came, and the largest concourse of people, ever seen in Texas, gathered. An attempt had been made to prevent the retiring president from delivering his valedictory address, the arrangements of the Inauguration Committee utterly excluded him. But when the fact was known, a burst of indignation went up from the vast multitude,—the Committee and their arrangements were all set aside, and the name of the Hero of San Jacinto was on every tongue.

When he came forward in the porch of the Capitol, and the people gazed upon his lofty, ample, and heroic form, relieved against the portrait of Washington, suspended behind him, a wild shout of enthusiasm rent the sky. He spoke three hours, and we have been told by those who heard him, that the dense thousands before him swayed to and fro under the impetuous storm of his eloquence, like a forest swayed by a strong wind. He had unrolled the scroll of the history of Texas—he portrayed her future policy, and dwelt upon her great destiny if that policy were pursued. He enjoined most solemnly good faith with all nations—economy in the government and in individuals—the cultivation of peace with the Indians—he warned the people against faction and the rancor of party spirit, and he implored them not to treasure up their hopes in annexation or treaties, but to rely upon their own public and private virtue—to be just and magnanimous with all men and with all nations.

And in conclusion, when he took his farewell of the people he loved, he extended his broad arms and poured down upon them from his great heart the benediction of the patriot and the soldier, as the tears streamed down his face. When he ceased, all was still but the deep murmur of subdued feeling, and that vast multitude was all in tears!

CHAPTER XI:
The Legislator

The new president began his administration by opposing everything that had been pursued and recommended by Houston. In his inaugural address he recommended the extermination of the Indians—pronounced a violent Philippic against annexation—advocated the establishment of a huge national bank, and inculcated a *splendid* government.

The first appropriation for frontier defense was one and a half million of Treasury Notes, and another half million for the civil list—without a dollar to base the issues upon. A regular army of two regiments was to be raised for exterminating the frontier tribes. A law was passed to remove the seat of government to some point northwest of the San Antonio Road. Commissioners were appointed by Congress from its own body, contrary to the constitution, to perform this act. The entire object of the movement was speculation. With land scrip, which they had procured, and certificates of headrights granted to settlers, they dispatched surveyors to locate land around the spot where Austin now stands—at the extremest settlement of the Republic even at this day. The expense of removal, with the erection of suitable buildings, caused an additional issue of promissory notes. The new capital was so far from the settlements the plank had to be carried thirty miles.

The Republic soon lost confidence in the administration—the depression of the currency naturally followed. And yet, in this state of embarrassment of the finances, and while Texas was at peace with Mexico, the president caused a proposition to be introduced into both Houses to conduct an expedition to Santa Fe, through a wilderness and prairie more than five hundred miles. The proposition was made in both Houses at the same time, and by both rejected. But the president ordered the expedition during the recess of Congress in 1840; and upwards of three hundred armed men started on a warlike expedition to a distant country. Its disasters are too well known to need a relation. The president appointed a governor for Santa Fe—a custom house officer and a military commandant, and organized a territorial government. All his plans subsequently fell into the hands of the enemy, when the men were captured, and were a moving cause for the cruelty with which they were treated. The expedition flooded the country with another enormous issue of paper "promises to pay money," unauthorized by the constitution or Congress. The horses on that expedition cost, on an average, a thousand dollars, the currency of the president had become so depreciated. Costly arms and munitions of war had been abstracted from the public arsenal by presidential edict—the country was robbed of a large number of its most chivalrous men—the public wagons and means of transportation were laid hold of, and a piece of artillery, with 'Mirabeau B. Lamar' inscribed on its breech, dragged through the prairies that immense distance to become the trophy of the enemies of Texas and afford an illustration of the stupidity of the president, and the degradation of the nation.

This expedition revived the hostilities between Texas and Mexico, which, but for it, would have slept, perhaps, forever. Houston had left the two countries really at peace, and the sole cause we have ever been able to ascertain for the renewal of hostilities was this silly and lamentable expedition. It is to be remarked, that for some time previous to this expedition, Mr. Lamar had sent commissioners to Gen. Arista, and his object is supposed, by his friends, to have been to propose a union of the northern provinces with Texas, forming a great power, over whose government he was to be placed. The sagacious Arista took advantage of the incompetency of his friend, and returned commissioners. They were in Austin when the Santa Fe Expedition took up its line of march, and witnessed the silly display. What passed between "the high contracting parties," is not known with certainty, for the facts have never been officially disclosed. The world knows the result. Arista seems to have given into the plan, for one thing is certain, the expedition started from Austin with a guide who had long resided in Mexico, and spoke the language perfectly; and the commanding officers charged him with their betrayal at San Miguel and Santa Fe. When the guide got them many days in the wilderness, and the miseries of their situation began to press heavily on them, he abandoned them in their calamity, and never was heard of again. The object of Arista doubtless was to have them conducted into the solitudes of the wilderness, and there left to perish—if this should fail, the authorities of Santa Fe, being duly informed, were to receive, betray and then capture them. The blame of all these proceedings is to be cast upon the president.

During his administration, he sent two ministers to Vera Cruz—but neither of them was received; and they returned, to the disgrace of Texas. There was no method or consistency in anything he did. That he wished to be distinguished and wished well to his adopted country, there is no doubt; but he was a feeble and puerile statesman. In civil affairs, he was a great schemer. One day, his hobby was a national bank; another, it was a great national road; a third, it was an alliance with Mexico, by his marrying the daughter of some distinguished public functionary of that country; for the diplomatist supposed his alliance with some opulent family would be tantamount to an alliance between the two nations. One day, he must make war upon one tribe of Indians; the next day, upon another. His first great exploit, when his administration began, was to attack the Cherokees, and drive them from their possessions between the Nueces and Sabine rivers, where they had been settled longer than the Texian colonists themselves. They had been invited by Mexico from the United States, and land had been assigned and great inducements held out to them. They had settled there, and were quietly and inoffensively pursuing their avocations. In 1835, the Consultation had

guaranteed to that tribe undisturbed possession of their territory, by a solemn assurance, signed by each member of the Consultation. A treaty had been subsequently made with the tribe (recognizing the same rights and guaranty) by Houston and other commissioners, and this treaty had been ratified by the Consultation. The Convention which declared their independence, had recognized this as well as all other acts of the Consultation as valid. A more solemn ratification of a treaty could not have been made.

Mr. Lamar began his administration by carrying out that section of his inaugural address, in which he had recommended the extermination of the Indians. The Cherokees were a peaceful, industrious and profitable community. The arts had made considerable progress among them, and they lived nearly as comfortably as white men. During the hostilities with Mexico, they had been prevented by the influence of Houston and Rusk from going over to the enemy, and they had made great advances in civilization during Houston's presidency. They looked upon the Texians as their friends, and Houston as their "Father." With a force of 700 men, a portion of whom had fought at San Jacinto, Lamar commenced his war of extermination against "Houston's pet Indians." His force was some five times superior, and of course he carried ruin to the poor red men's homes!

This treatment of the Cherokees and other tribes spread scenes of rapine and murder from the Red River to the Rio Grande. Even the president's two regiments of regulars in the field could not secure frontier protection.

In the disorders of Yucatan, when a separation from Mexico was spoken of, Mr. Lamar entered into a treaty of alliance with a minister sent to him for that purpose, and, without the concurrence of the Senate or the ratification of the treaty, ordered the Texian Navy to sail to the coast of Yucatan. That province was then an integral part or Mexico, and had not proclaimed revolt or independence.

Such were some of the acts of this puerile administration. We should not have glanced at them, even in so brief a manner, had it not been necessary to give the reader an idea of the state of the country when Houston's second term began. Lamar, who had found the government perfectly organized, had succeeded in reducing the country to the very verge of ruin. All the difficulties that had lain in the way of the advancement of Texas, Houston had successfully overcome. Disinterested and sagacious spectators of the progress of affairs beyond the Sabine, have often been heard to say, that in no portion of the world had a civil government ever been established and consolidated in so short a space of time. This was as much the work of Houston, as the victory of San Jacinto had been, although in both instances he was surrounded and aided by brave and true men, or he never could have done it. He left the domestic and foreign relations, the finances and the administration of law, the agriculture and the commerce of Texas, all in a sound, peaceful, flourishing state.

When Mr. Lamar left the administration, what was the state of the nation? He had committed outrages upon peaceful Indian tribes, and kindled the flames of savage war all along the borders of Texas. He had sent a hostile marauding expedition into the very heart of the Mexican provinces, and sent the navy to aid a revolting territory in making war upon Mexico, and now she was rousing all her force for a new invasion of Texas. He had quadrupled the national debt, and squandered the public treasure, till Texian securities depreciated ten to one. The people had lost all respect for the government, and confidence in its stability. The mail routes had been broken up, profligacy prevailed, and the social compact began to be regarded by the orderly and patriotic everywhere as virtually dissolved.

But Lamar's term had nearly expired, and the eyes of all men, who surveyed with gloomy forebodings the ruin that seemed to have fallen on the country, were now turned once more anxiously upon Houston. Even the lawless and the desperate began to fear the result of their crimes, and with one united voice the man, who had already twice saved the country, was called a third time to the helm. Houston was one of the few men who believed that the nation and the government could be saved, and he came forward to the rescue. No conventions were obliged to nominate him. There was an almost universal feeling that no other man could save Texas, and Texas made him her president for the second time, the very first hour the constitution would allow her.

During Lamar's administration Houston had consented to represent his district in the Congress of 1839-40, and again in 1840-41, and it was well that he had, for he not only arrested the tide of evil—*he had prevented a dissolution of the government.* On a certain occasion, after a stormy debate, Congress was going to adjourn *sine die.* The members publicly proclaimed that all hope of carrying on the government was gone, and they were determined to end the farce by going home. Houston rose in the midst of the tempest, as the members were leaving their seats, and addressed the Speaker. There never was a time when *that* man could not get a hearing, and the rush to the door stopped. "Let us hear old Sam," was the voice on every side.

The crowd began to return—members gradually resumed their seats and dropped their hats—they pressed up around him—the House became still, and not ten minutes went by before nothing was heard throughout the hall but the rich, deep voice that had echoed over the field of San Jacinto. No idea of the speech can be given but by telling the result. He closed by reading a resolution, "that the House adjourn till tomorrow morning at the usual hour," and not a member voted against it! They flocked around him, and so universal was the feeling that but for him the government would have gone to pieces, that even his old enemies seized him by the hand, and thanked him "for saving the country."

CHAPTER XII:
Again President

He was inaugurated the second time on the 13th of December, 1841. His message was hardly delivered before the news came of the capture of the Santa Fe Expedition. This was the first greeting he had, in office, of the fatal results of the policy of his predecessor. He, however, began immediately to bethink himself of the redemption of the unfortunate men who had been deluded away into the wilderness—for the lives of Texian soldiers seemed to be as dear to him as they could have been if they had been his own children.

The government was now in an infinitely worse state than it had been when he took the reins five years before. Then it was a formless chaos—now it was a *ruin*. The body politic had fallen into premature and inflammatory decay. It was not a disease only, but a *relapse*. The treasury was not only empty but millions in debt, and not another dollar could be borrowed in Christendom. The promissory notes and liabilities of the government depreciated *ten to one*, and they were *postponed*, but not *repudiated*. The money had been squandered, but the debt must be paid. But Texas could at that time have no more paid it than Parliament could pay the debt of England. But something had to be done. Houston proposed a new currency called the Exchequer System—its entire issues were not to exceed $200,000. He had asked as a guarantee for their redemption the customs of the country, and certain tracts of lands, amounting to about three millions of acres. While in Congress he had procured an act to be passed declaring these lands not subject to location. But now the private interests of members were to be interfered with, and although Congress hypothecated the customs they would not pledge the lands.

The president was fully aware of the opposition that was combining against him. The same hostile clique which had attempted to ruin him whenever he was in power, and who had come so near ruining the country when they had power themselves, were now determined to control the appointments under the new administration. But all attempts to constrain his policy proved as ineffectual as they had hitherto done. He chose for his cabinet officers men in whom he had unlimited confidence, and they were among the most enlightened and firm statesmen of Texas. Mr. Jones, the late president, became Secretary of State, Col. Hockley, a warm patriot and a devoted friend of Houston in all his struggles, Secretary of War and Marine, Wm. H. Dangerfield, Secretary of the Treasury, and G. W. Terrell, Attorney General. During these turbulent times, when prominent men declared openly that they would ruin Houston's administration, even if they had to do it by a revolution, multitudes of broken down speculators and politicians from the United States were continually flocking into Texas, and as they found little chance of winning distinction in the new field they had chosen, they joined the ranks of the opposition, and devoted themselves zealously to the ruin of the state.

But Houston had marked out his policy and he went calmly and firmly on to its execution. His first measure was to dispatch a minister to Washington to open negotiations for the annexation of Texas. His first object was annexation—if this failed, his next was the recognition of the independence of Texas by Mexico; and if he failed in both, he was resolved to open negotiations with France and England, and enter into some treaty or alliance which would secure peace to Texas, extend her commerce, and advance her prosperity. His next movement was to recall the navy, which Mr. Lamar had dispatched to help on a revolt in Yucatan.

In the meantime the country was absolutely stripped of all her defenses. A wide coast and a broad sea were open to the depredations of the enemy; the Santa Fe Expedition and the league with Yucatan had given Mexico every provocation for a renewal of hostilities; and the outrages committed upon the Indian tribes had broken the amity that had subsisted.

In this exposed situation of the country, when an irruption from the frontiers, or an invasion from Mexico, might be reasonably apprehended, Houston recommended Congress to raise a company of sixty men to protect the archives—for there was then no military force in the field. Congress refused to grant the subsidies necessary, and adjourned the 5th of February. He soon after started for Houston, to bring his family to the seat of government. While he was at Galveston, in the early part of March, the news came of the invasion by Vasquez. The intelligence spread the deepest alarm throughout the country. All along the western border, families were seen flying from their habitations towards the interior. The public mind was stirred by the wildest apprehensions. Everybody knew the provocation that had been given to the enemy—the follies and the disasters of Santa Fe seemed but a prelude to another Goliad or Alamo slaughter—the coast was without protection, and no army concentrated to march on the invader.

Suddenly all the intrigues and conspiracies against Houston ceased. The very men who had been foremost to threaten the overthrow of his administration in the storm of a revolution, were now the most active in stimulating their neighbors to prepare for the approaching disasters. Committees of vigilance and safety were everywhere organized, and all those means resorted to which are called into requisition in revolutionary times. Houston's orders at this time show that he did not believe the enemy would remain long in the country. The event proved that the Mexicans had already made a precipitate retreat beyond the Rio Grande, after committing outrages upon the citizens of San Antonio.

In the meantime, the press throughout the south and west had displayed great sympathy for the cause of Texas, and relying upon the sensation caused in the United States by the news of the reported invasion and the miscarriage of the Santa Fe expedition, Houston made an appeal to the American people. He sent agents to the United States to receive contributions, and procure volunteers. He issued a proclamation, in which he distinctly required that all troops which came should be perfectly armed and provisioned for a campaign of six months —since Texas had no means of doing it herself—several hundred volunteers went to Texas, in direct violation of the proclamation—for they went without arms and without provisions. Contributions were merely nominal. Some generous individuals in Georgia raised something over $500 at a public meeting —but all that was raised besides, throughout the United States, and reported to the government of Texas, in arms, ammunition, provisions, equipments and money, did not amount to five hundred dollars!

In June, Houston called an extra session of Congress, to consider the state of the country, and devise means for national defense. They debated and legislated without much formality or delay, for the impression was general, that if anything was to be done, it had better be done quickly. So, too, all wise men would have said, "if t'were *well* done." But their deliberations ended in passing a bill which invested Houston with dictatorial powers, and appropriated ten millions of acres of the public domain, to carry on a campaign. But this came no nearer making a provision for war, than a resolution appropriating ten millions of acres of blue sky, and conferring dictatorial power upon the north wind! For there was not a dollar of money in the treasury to pay agents to go and dispose of the land, and Houston was the last man to make use of dictatorial powers in resisting the encroachments of a dictator.

But Congress thought they had acquitted themselves like men—and their disposition, probably, was good enough too— but it had no more efficacy than the disposition of the man who willed in his last testament all his debts to be paid, for in neither case could the executor find anything had been left to pay the debts with. Apprehensions had been felt, while the bill was under debate, that Houston would veto it, and the time he could constitutionally keep it had nearly gone by. The excitement was intense; the capital was filled with angry and desperate men, and their noisy clamor spread over the country. All sorts of accusations were brought against the Executive, and he was plied with threats from every quarter. He was told that his life would pay the forfeit if he vetoed the bill. His friends, who apprehended his assassination, gathered around him, and besought him not to hazard a veto, for it would end in the ruin of himself and his country. At last the *ebullitions* of excitement began to subside, but they were followed by demonstrations of a deeper and more desperate feeling. For two weeks, few, even of his friends, approached the president's house, and they stole there under the shadow of the night;—assassins, in the meantime, were lurking around his dwelling. Even his cabinet officers began to talk about resigning.

But in the midst of all this storm, which few men could have resisted, Houston was calm and cheerful. He stationed no guard around his house; he had no spies on the alert; he did not even inquire what was said in Congress, or done in the streets. The blinds and the windows of his dwelling were wide open, and he was often seen walking across his parlor, conversing cheerfully with his family. His wife, whom he had married in 1840, and one of the most accomplished and gifted of women, reposed confidently upon his character, and she calmly and confidingly sustained him by her placid and intellectual conversations. Long after the lights had been extinguished through the town, and sullen, desperate, armed men were gathered in secret meetings to plot, and counter-plot, the gay voice of his wife, mingling with the tones of the harp and the piano, was heard coming forth from the open windows of Houston's dwelling.

All this must seem strange to the reader, without doubt, but we shall very soon solve the mystery. It was a tremendous crisis; but Houston was equal to it, and we know of no act of his life in which he gave such indubitable evidence that nature had lavished upon him all those gifts which make up the really great man. The reader, too, will agree with us.

When the time came, the veto was sent up to Congress. In it he showed that they had utterly and totally failed to accomplish the object for which he had called them together. They had proclaimed war against a powerful and organized foe, but they had made no provision for carrying it on. The president had not the means of buying a pound of powder. If they would provide the means for a campaign, he would head it himself, if necessary; but without money, no army could be made ready to take the field, and any attempt at hostilities would only bring down upon Texas universal contempt. He also dwelt upon the danger of the precedent they had established, in conferring upon the Chief Magistrate of the country unlimited powers. The prerogatives of a dictator he never would accept, while they were fighting against that same power in a neighboring state.

The veto was published,—a universal calm at once succeeded, and the man who had been covered with maledictions, became the idol of the people.

We are now obliged to cut short our relation of events in detail, to give a brief account of other more important movements. Confidence began to be restored. One open rebellion against the laws of the country Houston put down by going to the scene, and calling out the militia. When desperadoes found there was a man at the head of affairs, who could not be trifled with, they soon disbanded, and the supremacy of law was again restored. A new set of men were in office— justice was efficiently administered—economy was observed, and although Mr. Lamar had saddled an enormous debt upon the country, which could not be discharged for a long time to come, yet public credit was being restored, and men began to feel proud of their government.

Houston had left no resource untried to effect the liberation of the Santa Fe prisoners. He had appealed to all friendly powers to mediate in their release. The Congress of Texas had adjourned, after the news of their capture had arrived, without doing anything to aid the president in restoring them to their liberty. They had been given up as doomed men; they had gone to Santa Fe in violation of the law of nations, and with no constitutional authority from their government. They had been thrown on Houston's hands; his only reliance was on the terms of their capitulation, for he insisted that, even if they had been outlaws before, this had brought them within the pale of civilized warfare. We have, no space to give the history of the negotiations that were carried on for the release of these brave but misguided men. Suffice it to say, that they were liberated. Nor have we space to give the history of the Mier Expedition. Probably some authentic account (for none such has yet appeared) will one day be published.

Texas had now been repeatedly invaded by predatory Mexican bands, who seemed to have but two objects—to harass the nation they could not subdue, and pay up their arrearages due to their soldiers from the treasury of Mexico, with spoils of the robber. Mexico was always talking about a grand campaign, but since the Battle of San Jacinto she had not dared to meet the revolted province in honorable battle. The people of Mexico knew that the tyranny of her dictators had lost them forever that portion of their dominion; and at no period did they wear the yoke so tamely that the tyrant in power dared to leave the capital to head any army of invasion. Whoever that tyrant may have been, he knew that his worst enemies were the Mexicans themselves; his supremacy rested upon the presence of his troops in the city, and if he succeeded in consolidating his power at home, and turned his face towards Texas, he was sure to be overtaken by a courier from the capital with the news that his dominion was ended, and another dictator had been proclaimed. In the opinion of the Texian president, the time had come when the civilized world should interfere to end this contemptible system of pillage and robbery of the Republic.

Accordingly he caused his Secretary of State to address the following high toned and honorable appeal to the Great Powers, which had acknowledged the independence of Texas. It shows clearly the condition of Texas, and will correct many false impressions which have gone abroad in reference to the struggles of that nation. It is also proper to add, that this was the paper which proved so powerful in winning the sympathy and respect of Sir Robert Peel and M. Guizot, who ever after showed the deepest interest in the fortunes of Texas.

DEPARTMENT OF STATE, TEXAS.
Washington. October 15th, 1842.

I am instructed by his Excellency, the President, to submit for your consideration and action, a subject of general concern to civilized nations, but of peculiar interest to Texas, viz: the character of the war at present waged by Mexico against this country. The President is led to believe, from the nature of the facts involved, that this step will be deemed not only admissible but entirely proper. The civilized and Christian world are interested in the unimpaired preservation of those principles and rules of international intercourse, both in peace and war, which have received the impress of wisdom and humanity, and been strengthened, through a long course of time, by the practice and approval of the most powerful and enlightened of modern States. To these rules, in their application to the pending difficulties between this republic and Mexico, your attention is respectfully invited.

Whenever a people, separate and sovereign in their political character, are admitted into the great community of nations, they incur responsibilities and contract obligations which are reciprocal in their character, and naturally binding upon all the members of this community, the extent and force of which depend upon that code of ethics which prescribes the reciprocal duties and obligations of each sovereign member. Hence arises the right to control the mode of warfare pursued by one nation toward another, and the corresponding duty of providing against the perpetration of acts at variance with the laws of humanity, and the settled usages of civilized nations.

In view of the character of hostilities, at present waged by Mexico against Texas, and of those principles which have been, in the opinion of this government, so frequently and so flagrantly violated by our enemy, the hope is confidently indulged by the President, that the direct interference of nations mutually friendly will be extended to arrest a species of warfare, unbecoming the age in which we live, and disgraceful to any people professing to be civilized.

The course of conduct uniformly observed by the government and people of Texas towards our enemy, stands in palpable contrast with their manifold enormities and wanton aggression, and will, it is confidently expected, furnish abundant ground for the exercise of the right of interference now invoked.

It has now been nearly seven years since the Declaration and the establishment of the Independence of this Republic. During the whole of this time, Mexico, although uniformly asserting the ability and determination to re-subjugate the country, has never made a formidable effort to do so. Her principal war has consisted of silly taunts and idle threats, of braggadocio bulletins and gasconading proclamations. All her boasted threats of invasion have resulted in nothing more than fitting out and sending into the most exposed portions of our territory, petty marauding parties for the purpose of pillaging and harassing the weak and isolated settlements on our western border.

Since March last, no less than three incursions of that character have been made, none of which have continued longer than eight days. The first party was composed of artillery, infantry, rancheros, and Indian warriors, in all about 700. Their attack was made upon the defenseless town of San Antonio. The second, consisting of about 800, attacked a party of about 200 emigrants at Lipantitlan. They were repulsed with loss and retreated out of the country. The last, under Gen. Woll, of about 1,300, attacked and took San Antonio the second time by surprise, during the session of the District Court. His force was composed of regulars, rancheros and Indians. The Indians employed by the Mexicans are fragments of bands originally from the United States, but now located within the limits of Texas. This government has always refused to employ the services of Indians, when tendered against Mexico, and has sought every possible means to mitigate, rather than increase the calamities of war.

Persisting in this effort, the President has had recourse to the present measure, with a hope to subserve the cause of humanity. Should this effort fail, the government must resort to retaliatory measures, growing out of our peculiar situation, which are to be deprecated by every Christian and generous feeling. The rulers of nations are responsible for their preservation, and as a last resort, must adopt a just retaliation. What is most to be deplored in a war of this character, is, that the unoffending and defenseless become victims of the most relentless cruelty. War, in its most generous and noble aspect, is accompanied by great calamities, nations are not benefited by it, and it must be productive of great individual sufferings. But when individuals and nations are exasperated by repeated wrongs, even cruelty itself may be rendered tolerable, if it be used as retaliation for injuries long endured. The massacres and cruelties which have been inflicted upon Texas, since the commencement of her revolution, have been responded to by a generous forbearance, but that cannot be expected longer to exist.

The object of Mexico, in her course, cannot be misunderstood. By incursions of the character complained of, the spirits of our husbandmen and farmers are depressed—the cry of invasion is kept up, and the excitement incidental to war prevents emigration, and embarrasses our resources, by deterring men of enterprise and capital from making importations of goods into our country. This, for a time, may avail her something, but the aggregate of human suffering will be a poor recompense for the advantages she may gain. The origin, genius, and character of the people of Texas, are guarantees for her ultimate success. Nations that contribute to her advancement will command her gratitude. Never, since 1836, has Mexico attempted anything like a general invasion of the country, or conducted the war upon any plan calculated to test the superiority of the two nations on the field of battle, and bring the war to a close by the arbitration of arms. Her hostile demonstrations, thus far, have consisted, exclusively, in the clandestine approach of small bands of rancheros from the valley of the Rio Grande, for plunder and theft, but sometimes associated with fragments of the Mexican army, composed for the most part of convict soldiery, fit for nothing either honorable in enterprise or magnanimous in conduct. The people of Texas, being, for the most part, agriculturalists, engaged in the tillage of the soil, the consequences of this predatory system of warfare have been to them extremely vexatious and harassing, without in any degree hastening the adjustment of the difficulties existing between the parties. Entirely different is the general character of the Mexican population. They are literally a nation of herdsmen, subsisting, in a great measure, on the proceeds of their flocks and herds. They can move about from place to place, and make their homes wherever inclination or convenience may prompt, without detriment.

Hitherto the conduct and disposition of the Government and people of Mexico have been diametrically opposed to those manifested by the people of Texas. While the one has been depredating upon the property and dwellings of our exposed and defenseless frontier, murdering the inhabitants in cold blood, or forcing them away into a loathsome, and too often fatal, captivity; inciting the murderous tribes of hostile Indians, who reside along our northern border, to plunder our exposed settlements, stimulating to the most cruel and barbarous massacres, and inhuman butcheries, even of our defenseless women and children, and to commit every excess of savage warfare—the other, animated by the hope of a further resort to arms and their attendant calamities, for injuries received, returned forbearance.

The President has sought to abstain from the effusion of blood, and in that aim has uniformly restrained the impetuosity and calmed the excitement of his countrymen, so often aroused by a course of conduct which violates every rite both private and national, and a cruelty and depravity which would disgrace the darkest ages of feudal barbarism. The popular impulse might have been turned upon the enemy, on their own soil. The result might have proved that a free people, burning with vengeance long restrained, could levy a heavy retaliation.

Such being the character of hostile operations against Texas, on the part of our enemy, which being plainly violative of every principle of civilized or honorable warfare, and, at the same time, so little calculated to achieve the professed object of the war—the re-conquest of Texas, the President confidently hopes the Government of _____ will feel not only justified, but even called upon, to interpose its high authority and arrest their course of proceedings, and require of Mexico either the recognition of the Independence of Texas, or to make war upon her according to the rules established and universally recognized by civilized nations. If Mexico believes herself able to re-subjugate this country, her right to make the effort to do so is not denied, for, on the contrary, if she choose to invade our territory with that purpose, the President, in the name of the people of all Texas, will bid her welcome. It is not against a war with Mexico that Texas would protest. This she deprecates not. She is willing at any time to stake her existence as a nation upon the issue of a war conducted on Christian principles. It is alone against the unholy, inhuman, and fruitless character it has assumed, and still maintains, which violates every rule of honorable warfare, every precept of religion, and sets at defiance even the common sentiments of humanity, against which she protests, and invokes the interposition of those powerful nations which have recognized her independence. The Government of this Republic has already given an earnest of its disposition to consult the wishes of other nations, when those wishes do not conflict with the general interests and convenience of the country. Fully appreciating

the friendly sentiments of those Powers, which have acknowledged the Independence of Texas, and relying much upon
their ability and influence in securing an early and permanent adjustment of our difficulties with Mexico, the President,
in compliance with the desire of those Nations, expressed
through their Representatives to this Government, revoked
the late proclamation of blockade against Mexico, and thus
removed every cause of embarrassment to those nations in
their intercourse with our enemy. Having thus yielded the opportunity of retaliating upon our enemy the many injuries we
have received at her hands, the President feels less reluctance
in making this representation, and invoking the interposition
of those nations to put an end to a mode of warfare at once
disgraceful to the age, so evil in its consequences to civil society, so revolting to every precept of the Christian religion, and
shocking to every sentiment of humanity.

G. W. TERRELL,
Attorney General & Acting Secretary of State

CHAPTER XIII:

ANNEXATION—FRENCH, BRITISH & AMERICAN CABINETS

This luminous and able paper unfolded clearly the merits of the Texian struggle, and it received the profound attention of the cabinets of Washington, London, and Paris. The leading journals of England and France, borrowing their prejudices and their intelligence about Texian affairs from powerful and widely circulated American papers, had hitherto regarded the people of Texas as a band of outlaws. Scarcely a word of encouragement or sympathy had been uttered by their ministers to the agents of Texas in Europe, and beyond a tardy recognition of her independence, they hardly ventured. The American press groaned under the burden of calumnies against the Texian people and their bold leader.

Consequently, this appeal was received and read with surprise and mortification. They saw that the same high veneration for justice—the same lofty regard for national honor, and the same (if not a nobler) recognition of the claims of humanity and Christian principle which had characterized the progress and the intercourse of those great kingdoms—inspired the councils of the man who had given freedom to his outraged country.

We have been told, and we do not doubt it, that both of those great ministers, who guided the destinies of England, declared, on reading this appeal, that it would have done honor to the bravest nation and most enlightened statesmen. However this may have been, we do know, from the archives of Texas, that immediately afterward a rivalry began between the French and English cabinets, for the cultivation of friendly relations with Texas. Instructions were sent to the ministers of those nations accredited to the Texian government, to allow no opportunity of winning the regard and friendship of the Republic to pass unimproved. We also know, too, that no effort which vigilant ministers could put forth, and no motives which keen-sighted diplomatists could press, were left untried, to gain for their sovereigns control over the commerce and the political fortunes of Texas. They saw that as an independent power, no barriers could be interposed to her ultimate advancement; and it became a matter of infinite moment to France and England, to prevent the final union of Texas with the United States. Hence, those powers watched with so much vigilance and alarm, the tendency of affairs towards annexation. Hence, they brought into requisition all their diplomatic, commercial and financial machinery to prevent what they clearly foresaw would prove so detrimental a blow to all their interests in the New World. We have had facilities for knowing something of these movements, and we venture to say, that had not Houston had the control of these negotiations, and had he not been a man whose policy neither England nor France could constrain or coerce by any motives of personal aggrandizement—Texas never would have been a part of our confederacy, and those great powers would have gained a foothold beyond the Sabine, which would not unlikely have transferred to their hands that vast empire which we are yet to wield towards the shores of the Pacific.

The very moment the French and British cabinets saw the tendency of events, they increased their vigilance just in proportion as Texas was spurned from our embraces. But while timidity and apprehensions filled the minds of the friends of Texas in this country, and Congress, blinded by falsehood and prejudice, plied by threats and awed by clamor, still held itself aloof from all legislation on the subject, Mr. Tyler and his cabinet were no idle spectators of the advancing drama. That president, whatever may have been the wisdom of the rest of his course, pursued in the affair of Texas a most enlightened, sagacious, and American policy. He saw the vast importance of consummating annexation at the earliest possible moment, and what vigilance, activity, and a complete understanding of the merits of the question could accomplish, was done. His efforts were at last successful. And although his reputation as a statesman may have suffered, and he may have paid the penalty of having in many things proved untrue to both parties as well as to himself, yet all these things will be in a great measure forgotten, and the time will come when the vast consequences of that great act, whose consummation is so much due to him, will become so apparent to all our people, that his name will be cherished by every American. Throughout his administration, he was true to his policy on this question. Unawed by popular clamor, and unseduced by the minions who pressed around his feet (and who brought the eclipse over his fame), he steadily and firmly pursued his noble purpose.

In the meantime France and England *did* interfere, and brought about an armistice between Mexico and Texas. The friendly offices of our cabinet were also proffered, but they had little influence with Mexico. The negotiations in London were conducted with consummate ability by Mr. Ashbel Smith.

In a dispatch from the Department of State of Texas, to Mr. Van Zandt, Charge d'Affaires of the Republic at Washington, dated July 6th, 1843, that functionary was thus instructed: "The United States having taken no definite action in this matter, and there now being an increased prospect of an adjustment of our difficulties with Mexico, the President deems it advisable to take no further action at present in reference to annexation, but has decided to await the issue of events now in progress, and to postpone that subject for future consideration, and for such action as circumstances may hereafter render most expedient for the interests of this country."

This extract, with others we shall presently give, will unfold what has been a matter of so much dispute, viz.:—the policy of Houston on this important subject. Whatever his own private feelings may have been, it was exceedingly doubtful whether our government would ever consent to annexation on what he considered fair and equal terms; and he was resolved to maintain with France and England the most friendly relations; that in the event of Texas being spurned from the embrace of the United States, she might fall back upon a treaty with a powerful ally, under whose patronage she might claim protection from her foe, and under whose policy (made liberal by interest) she might advance rapidly to power.

The French and English ministers resident in Texas, had already manifested some little jealousy on the subject of Houston's negotiations with the Washington cabinet, and seeing little probability of consummating a treaty of annexation, he instructed Mr. Van Zandt to defer all further action for the time being.

Accordingly, instructions were forwarded to Mr. Van Zandt on the 13th of December, 1843. The following extracts will clearly unfold the reasons for Houston's policy.

> The interposition of foreign friendly governments, by which an Armistice has been established between Texas and Mexico, and the prospect of a permanent peace with that power given, has been extended by the particular governments mostly influential in obtaining these most desirable results chiefly with a view that, in the event of Mexico's agreeing to acknowledge the independence of Texas, she should continue to exist as a separate and independent nation. The great object and desire of Texas is the establishment of a permanent and satisfactory peace with her enemy, and for this purpose the good offices of these powers have been asked and obtained, and the object sought for, through their intervention, appears now on the eve of being realized.

> This intervention and these good offices have been gratuitously and unconditionally given, and although Texas is entirely free to pursue any course she may please in future, the President thinks that, in the present state of our foreign relations, it would not be politic to abandon the expectations which now exist of a speedy settlement of our difficulties with Mexico through the good offices of other powers, for the very uncertain prospect of annexation to the United States, however desirable that event,

if it could be consummated, might be. Were Texas to agree to a treaty of annexation, the good offices of these powers would, it is believed, be immediately withdrawn, and were the treaty then to fail of ratification by the Senate of the United States, Texas would be placed in a much worse situation, than she is at present, nor could she again ask or hope for any interposition in her behalf, either by England or France; and with our consequent supposed dependence upon the United States, might again return the apathy and indifference towards us which has always until now characterized that government. Texas would then be left in the same situation she was two years since, without a friend, and her difficulties with Mexico unsettled.

This government is duly sensible of the very friendly feelings evinced by the President of the United States, in the offer to conclude a treaty for the annexation of this country, but from all the information which he has been able to obtain in relation to the views and feelings of the people of the United States, he is induced to believe that its approval by the other branches of that government would be, if not refused, at least of very uncertain attainment at this particular time—therefore, and until such an expression of their opinion can be obtained as would render this measure certain of success, the President deems it most proper and most advantageous to the interests of this country, to decline the proposition for concluding a treaty. In making a communication of this determination to the government of the United States, it will be proper to inform that government that whenever the Congress or Senate of the United States shall throw wide open the door to annexation by a resolution authorizing the President of that country to propose a treaty for the purpose, the proposition will be immediately submitted to the representatives of the people of this country, and promptly responded to on the part of its government.

The present determination of the President on this subject, does not proceed from any change in his views of the general policy of the measure, *but from a change in the relations of this country with other powers.*

These instructions to suspend negotiations on the subject of annexation, with a knowledge that England was pressing her powerful and friendly offices upon the Republic, alarmed the cabinet at Washington. The facts which were soon after made public excited the apprehensions also, not only of all the friends of annexation, but of all those Americans, who had the foresight to anticipate the prejudicial consequences that would come upon this country by allowing England to gain a foothold on our southern frontier. She had always proved a bad neighbor, as our difficulties growing out of the north-eastern and Oregon boundaries had abundantly proved, and the deepest anxiety was everywhere manifested for the prompt action of Congress. In the meantime, Mr. Tyler, fearing the result, had instructed his Secretary of State to lose no opportunity of assuring the Texian government of his earnest desire to consummate annexation. The president of Texas was placed in a position of extreme delicacy, and any imprudent act or movement would have proved exceedingly hazardous to the interests of his country. He had early manifested his desire for annexation, and done all he could to effect it during his first executive term. Under Mr. Lamar's administration, the question had slept. Houston had pursued a discreet course in regard to it after his re-election, and although he had now been for some time earnestly occupied in securing annexation, he had, like a wise man, kept his own counsels.

On the 20th of January, 1844, however, he sent a secret message to Congress, in which he used the following language:

Connected with our present condition, our foreign relations are becoming daily more and more interesting; and it seems to me that the representatives of the people should anticipate the events which may in all probability occur...The Executive, therefore, relies upon the deliberative wisdom and decision of the representatives of the people to give him all the aid in their power to conduct the affairs of Texas to such an issue as will be promotive of its interests as a community, and at the same time gratifying to the people. Heretofore, he has carefully abstained, during his present administration, from the expression of any opinion in reference to the subject of annexation to the United States. And, in submitting this communication, he does not think it becoming in him now to express any preference.

It will be perceived by the honorable Congress, that if any effort were made on the part of this Government to effect the object of annexation, which is so desirable, and it should fail of meeting responsive and corresponding action on the part of the United States, it might have a seriously prejudicial influence upon the course which England and France might otherwise be disposed to take in our favor. And a failure on our part, after a decided expression, could not but be mortifying to us, and to a great extent diminish our claims to the confidence of other nations. It would create distrust on their part towards us; because the opponents of our interests would allege there was no stability in our purposes, and therefore unsafe in other nations to cultivate very intimate relations with us, or even to maintain those which now so fortunately exist. They might apprehend that after the lapse of a few more years, Texas, once having acquired increased importance from their friendly aid and good offices, would be induced again, by the agitation of the same question in the United States, to apply for admission into that Union, and that by possibility it might be effected. Hence the utmost caution and secresy on our part as to the true motives of our policy should be carefully observed.

He recommends that in the event of the failure of Texas, she should enter into "a treaty of alliance, defensive at least, if not offensive" with the United States.

"If nothing else," says he, "were effected in a treaty for defence, it would secure to Texas a position that would forever bid defiance to our Mexican enemy. It would be as important to us in fact as the recognition of our independence by Mexico."

He also proposes the appointment of "an additional agent to the Government of the United States, to co-operate with our agent there." He thus concludes:

If the honorable Congress should think well of these sugges-tions, they will be aware of the propriety of immediate action on the subject. The Congress of the United States have now been in session some time, and there can be but little doubt that if they have not already done so, they will soon indicate their disposition, and course of policy towards this country.

Believing as the Executive did, at the commencement of the present session, that the subject of annexation was in the best position in which Texas could place it, he did not allude to it in his general message—apprehending that any public action taken either by the Executive or the Congress would only have a tendency to embarrass the subject. Action must now be tak-en by the United States; and we must now watch and meet their disposition towards us.

If we evince too much anxiety, it will be regarded as impor-tunity, and the voice of supplication seldom commands great respect.

The spirit of this message inspired all Houston's acts on this great question, and the effect was most salutary. For it is more than probable that our Congress would have turned a deaf ear to "the voice of supplication," had they not discovered that the people of Texas, grown weary of delays and indignant at repeated repulses, would supplicate no longer. The position of parties was suddenly changed—completely reversed. It be-came clearer than noon-day, that unless Texas was allowed to come into our Union, under auspices the most favorable to her, she would not enter, and in any event it seemed probable that she was after all to be the sufferer. Her anxiety, therefore, for annexation, was every hour growing less, while ours was increasing.

Both parties were conscious of the movements of England —and while Texas saw in the extension of that proud shield over her young Republic, the boon of mighty protection, we watched with jealous and anxious interest the progress of that same imperial emblem. When, therefore, that Republic, whose people, "bone of our bone and flesh of our flesh," had been pleading on their knees the same admission which had hitherto been cordially tendered by Congress to every other American colony on the continent, was repulsed "like some stranger," she sprung to her feet, and the next moment we saw her youthful figure relieved against the giant form of Old England, whose purple mantle was thrown kindly over her shoulder, and whose flag of St. George was waving over her head. It was a strange, but beautiful spectacle. "Is that," said all, "the suppliant who so lately was kneeling on the steps of our Capitol?"

Texas was now lost to America. The only question was, "Can she be again won?" and the American Congress was no longer the sole party to answer the inquiry.

The cabinet at Washington manifested an anxiety to renew negotiations. In his letter to Mr. Van Zandt (29th Jan., 1844), Houston instructs his Minister to meet the United States halfway, and to inform him of any disposition on their part to come to the terms they had rejected. "They must be convinced," says he, "that England has rendered most important service to Texas by her mediatorial influence with Mexico." He then proceeds:

> If the United States really intend to deprive England of connections on this continent, a treaty of alliance, offensive and defensive, formed with this country against Mexico, would enable that government to retain an influence in the affairs of Texas which could be done by no other circumstance. In November, 1842, when Texas protested to the three Great Powers against the course pursued by Mexico in her war with this country, it was understood the three Powers were to act in harmony, so far as any mediation was to be interposed. From some circumstances, England appears to have been most active and efficient in her efforts. The United States, from their continuity in situation, had greater facilities than England at their command, and had they been as forward in their efforts at mediation as England, it would have been more grateful to the citizens of Texas. A moment's reflection will present many

reasons why it should have been so. When an individual is overwhelmed by misfortune, and that misfortune is lightened or relieved, the beneficiary always feels grateful for the benefits conferred; and in the event of a recurrence, would naturally look to the same source for a renewal of favor. Thus must it be with nations, and it requires no argument to convince the United States, that in submitting the first proposition for a treaty of alliance with them, the authorities of Texas are far from pretermitting any just claims which they may have to the confidence of Texas as a nation, but the reverse.

It is true that our eyes were directed to the United States, not only as a people but as a government, to which Texas was most willing to feel herself obligated. If we did not realize all our expectations, we are far from concluding that anything left unaccomplished by her arose from hostility to Texas on her part and for that, among other reasons, we propose an alliance as an earnest of the confidence we are still willing to place upon them and their efforts.

Negotiations were now once more commenced in earnest, and the two Ministers of Texas (Mr. Van Zandt, and Gen. Henderson, now Governor or Texas), represented their country with great ability, and won for themselves universal respect.

In the dispatch of Houston to Mr. Van Zandt (Feb. 15, 1844), informing him of the investment of Gen. Henderson (just appointed) and himself, "with proper powers to conclude the subject of annexation as far as it can be consummated by the Government of the United States and our Ministers," the president thus speaks of the vast consequences of annexation, if it should be effected. He continued:

It would be useless for me to attempt to portray to you the magnitude of the consequences which are to grow out of these transactions. Millions will realize the benefits; but it is not within the compass of mortal expression to estimate the advantages to mankind. The measures of this Government have not been devised without due consideration of the subject, so far as Texas may be affected by it; and no matter how great the ultimate advantages to the two countries may have been considered, in the event of annexation, it was the manifest duty of this Government to use such precaution as would secure it against any accidental catastrophe. It is now in possession of such assurances from the United States as will hazard the die.

In another dispatch, dated the 29th of April, 1844, we find the following language:—

I have felt, and yet feel, great solicitude for our fate. The crisis to Texas is everything. To the United States it is worth its union. My toil has constantly been for the freedom and happiness of mankind, and if we are annexed, I hope we shall have accomplished much; but if from any cause we should be rejected we must redouble our energies, and the accompanying duplicate will express to you decisively what my purposes are. Texas can become sovereign and independent, established upon her own incalculable advantages of situation, and sustained by European influences, without the slightest compromittal of her nationality. If the present measure of annexation should fail entirely, and we are to be thrown back upon our own resources, fix your eye steadily on the salvation of Texas, and pursue the course which I have indicated. I again declare to you, that every day which passes only convinces me more clearly that it is the last effort at annexation that Texas will ever make; nor do I believe that any solicitation or guarantee from the United States would, at any future day, induce her to consent to the measure.

But the Mission of General Henderson seemed likely to secure no good results, and in a dispatch of May 17th, 1844, he was advised to return. The President says:—

Whatever the desires of this Government, or the people, are, or might have been, in relation to Annexation, I am satisfied they are not ambitious, at this time, nor will ever be again, to be seen in the attitude of a bone of contention, to be worried or gnawed by conflicting politicians. The views of the Executive of this country, as well as the views of its citizens, were fairly presented in a willingness to become annexed to the United States. And though the advantages presented to the United States were incalculably greater than those resulting to Texas, she was willing to stand the hazard of the adventure.

The statesmen of that country appear to be united in opinion adverse to our admission into the Union of the North. We must, therefore, regard ourselves as a nation, to remain *forever separate.* It would be unpleasant for us to enter into a community, as a member, where we should be regarded ungraciously by either of the political parties. Texas, alone, can well be sustained, and no matter what sincere desire we may have entertained for a connection with that Government, and the affectionate enthusiasm that has existed in this towards it, we will be compelled to reconcile ourselves to our present condition, or to assume such an attitude towards other countries as will certainly look to our independence. This can be accomplished, if the United States will carry out the pledges which they have already given. The compromittal of our national honor I cannot contemplate, nor would I entertain any proposition which would be averse to our character as an independent nation; but Texas can now command interests which will require no such sacrifice. We must act!! ...It would seem, from the complexion of matter at Washington, that General Henderson's remaining there longer would be unnecessary. As indicated in my last communication, *negotiations can be very well conducted at this Government,* not designing to cut any reflections upon the representatives of this Government at Washington, in whom the Executive has the highest confidence. Moments of leisure could be employed here, and even hours and days commanded, which is not permitted when urgent dispatches arrive. The locality of our seat of Government is such, that the Executive has had to substitute himself in correspondence for the Secretary of State, and dispense with the services of that valuable officer, for the sake of dispatch. ...The measure of Annexation having been taken up at the instance of the United States, ought to secure Texas, and fortify her against all inconveniences arising from having opened negotiations on that subject. The treaty having been signed and submitted to the Senate, is all that can be performed on the part of Texas. Further solicitation, on her part, would present her as an object of commiseration to the civilized world. If the embarrassments of our condition have presented us in a humiliating posture, it furnishes no excuse to us for voluntary degradation.

Therefore it is, that my purpose is fixed in relation to the subject of which I have treated. The desires of the people of Texas, with my love of repose (thus far I am selfish), had determined me in favor of annexation. My judgment, though rendered subservient to their inclinations and my own has never fully satisfied the course adopted. Yet, in all good faith, I have lent and afforded every aid to its consummation.

We shall now close our extracts from Houston's dispatches by giving a portion of a very important private letter to Mr. Murphy, the American Minister to the Texian Government. We have nowhere seen the same views expressed in regard to the future destiny of Texas. The letter shows, beyond a question, that the writer was persuaded that Texas, even if she was compelled to stand alone, had no mean destiny awaiting her in the future. The views here given are those of a statesman—of one who knew the history of his nation and the character of her people—of a patriot, who never despaired for his country, before whose altars he had consecrated himself forever:

The times are big with coming events to Texas and the world. I feel that matters now transacting are, if carried out, to perpetuate the union of the States, by the Annexation of Texas, for centuries. If this great measure fails, the Union will be endangered; its revenues diminished; and a European influence will grow up in Texas, from our necessities and interests, that will most effectually prejudice the interests of the United States, so far as they are to look for the sale of their fabrics in the southern section of this continent, and a forfeiture of our sympathies. Mexico, in a short time, by the influences which Texas can command, will yield everything to the superior energy, activity, and the employment of well-directed capital, which will flow into us from Europe, and render us the beneficiaries of a most important and extensive trade. All our ports will soon become great commercial marts; and places, now scarcely noticed upon our maps, will be built up, and grow into splendid cities.

These are but few of the advantages which are noticed; but these, to the statesmen of the United States, ought to cause ceaseless efforts to secure so rich a prize.

The present moment is the only one that the United States will ever enjoy to annex Texas. I am intensely solicitous to see the matter consummated, and my country at rest. 'Tis true that we are not to be great gainers, when compared to the United States, in what they derive. Had I been at Washington, I would most certainly not have made a treaty so indefinite as to individual rights which may arise, and be involved in the subject of annexation. We surrender everything, and in reality get nothing but protection—and that at the hazard of being invaded or annoyed by Mexico before any aid could be rendered by the United States. I hope that the precautions taken will be such as to deter Mexico from any attempt upon us.

The fact, that the United States is one of the rival powers of the world, will render that nation more liable to war than we would be as a minor power. There are a thousand reasons which I could urge, why Texas would be more secure from trouble if she could have present peace,—which she can obtain readily if she is not annexed. When we once become a part and parcel of the United States we are subject to all their vicissitudes. Their commercial relations are extensive, which subjects them to jealousy and the rivalry of other powers, who will seek to overreach them, and cramp them by restrictions, or annoy them by interference. They will not be willing to submit to these things, and the consequences will be war. Nor will this danger arise from any one power of the earth, but from various nations. The wealth of European nations depends more upon their labor, than the people of this continent. We look to the soil—they to their manufacturing capacity, for the means of life as well as wealth. These facts are not all; and, indeed, but a very partial notice of important affairs. The political relations of the United States will increase, and become more complicated and extensive with their increase of power. Not only this, but they, too, will grow arrogant; and it will not be a half century, if the Union should last, until they feel a strong inclination to possess, by force, that which they at present would be willing to make a subject of negotiation and treaty.

In all consequences, if we are annexed, we have to bear a part of their troubles—no matter of what character. Alone and independent, Texas would be enabled to stand aloof from all matters unconnected with her existence as a nation; while the causes of war to the United States would be a source of benefit and prosperity to her. War could grow up between no power and the United States, but what Texas would be the beneficiary. The value of her staples would be enhanced, and that arising from the influence of war upon the United States. Texas, enjoying as she does a situation on the Gulf, and a neutral attitude, would derive the greatest possible benefits. Calamity to other nations would be wealth and power to Texas. The encouragement given us by the demand for our staples would increase our individual, as well as our national wealth. The fleets of belligerents would be supplied with meats from our natural pastures; and the sale of our superabundant herds would, when added to the sale of our other commodities, give us more wealth than any other nation, in comparison to our population.

Apart from this, if we should not be annexed, all the European nations would introduce with alacrity vast numbers of emigrants, because it would enable them to extend their commerce. Those who migrate from the different nations to Texas will retain predilections, for many years, in favor of the partialities which nativity carries with it in after life.

That France and England will pour into our country vast numbers of industrious citizens, there can be no doubt. Belgium, Holland, and other countries, will not be remiss in their duty to ulterior consequences. All these countries have an excess of population, and the common policy and economy of nations are such, that they will have a care to the location of those who leave their native countries. Never, to my apprehension, have all nations evinced the same disposition to commerce as that which is now exercised and entertained. Hence, no time has ever been so propitious for the upbuilding of a nation possessed of our advantages, as that which Texas at this moment enjoys, in the even to that the measure of annexation should fail. Its failure can only result from selfishness on the part of the Government or Congress of the United States. If faction, or a regard to present party advantages, should defeat the measure, you may depend upon one thing—and that is, that the glory of the United States has already culminated. A rival power will soon be built up, and the Pacific, as well as the Atlantic, will be component parts of Texas, in thirty years from this date.

The Oregon region, in geographical affinity, will attach to Texas. By this coalition, or union, the barrier of the Rocky Mountains will be dispensed with or obviated. England and France, in anticipation of such an event, would not be so tenacious on the subject of Oregon, as if the United States were to be the sole possessors of it. When such an event would take place, or in anticipation of such a result, all the powers, which either envy or fear the United States, would use all reasonable exertions to build us up, as the only rival power which can exist on this continent to that of the United States. Considering our origin, these speculations may seem chimerical, and that such things cannot take place. A common origin has its influence so long as a common interest exists, and no longer. Sentiment tells well in love matters or in a speech; but in the affairs and transactions of nations there is no sentiment or feeling but one, and that is essentially selfish.

I regard nations as corporations on a large and sometimes magnificent scale, but no more than this; consequently, they have no soul, and recognize no Mentor but interest.

Texas, once set apart and rejected by the United States, would feel that she was of humble origin; and if a prospect was once presented to her of becoming a rival to the United States it would only stimulate her to feelings of emulation; and it would be her least consideration, that, by her growth to power, she would overcome the humility of her early condition. So the very causes which now operate with Texas, and incline her to annexation, may, at some future period, give origin to the most active and powerful animosity between the two countries. This, too, we must look at, for it will be the case. Whenever difficulties arise between the United States and Texas, if they are to remain two distinct nations, the powers of Europe will not look upon our affairs with indifference; and no matter what their professions may be of neutrality, they can always find means of evasion. The union of Oregon and Texas will be much more natural and convenient than for either, separately, to belong to the United States. This, too, would place Mexico at the mercy of such a power as Oregon and Texas would form. Such an event may appear fanciful to many, but I assure you there are no Rocky Mountains interposing to such a project. But one thing can prevent its accomplishment, and that is annexation.

If you, or any Statesman, will only regard the map of North America, you will perceive that, from the 46th degree of latitude North, there is the commencement of a natural boundary. This will embrace the Oregon, and from thence south on the Pacific coast, to the 29th or 30th degree of south latitude, will be a natural and convenient extent of sea-board.

I am free to admit, that most of the Provinces of Chihuahua, Sonora, and the Upper and Lower Californias, as well as Santa Fe, which we now claim, will have to be brought into the connection of Texas and Oregon. This, you will see by reference to the map, is no bugbear to those who will reflect upon the achievements of the Anglo-Saxon people. What have they ever attempted, and recoiled from, in submission to defeat? Nothing, I would answer. Population would be all that would be needful, for, with it, resources would be afforded for the accomplishment of any enterprise. As to the proposition that the Provinces of Mexico would have to be overrun, there is nothing in this; for you may rely upon the fact that the Mexicans only require kind and humane masters to make them a happy people, and secure them against the savage hordes who harass them constantly, and bear their women and children into bondage. Secure them from these calamities, and they would bless any power that would grant them such a boon.

The Rocky Mountains interposing between Missouri and Oregon will very naturally separate them from the United States, when they see the advantages arising from a connection with another nation of the same language and habits with themselves. The line of Texas running with the Arkansas, and extending to the great desert, would mark a natural boundary between Texas, or a new and vast Republic to the Southwest. If this ever take place, you may rely upon one thing, which is this, that a nation, embracing the advantages of the extent of seventeen degrees on the Pacific, and so extensive a front on the Atlantic as Texas does, will not be less than a rival power to any of the nations now in existence.

You need not estimate the population, which is said, or reputed, to occupy the vast Territory embraced between the 29th and 46th degrees of latitude on the Pacific. They will, like the Indian race, yield to the advance of the North American population. The amalgamation, under the guidance of statesmen, cannot fail to produce the result, in creating a united Government, formed of, and embracing the limits suggested.

It may be urged that these matters are remote. Be it so. Statesmen are intended by their forecast to regulate and arrange matters in such sort as will give direction to events by which the future is to be benefited or prejudiced.

You may freely rely, my friend, that future ages will profit by these facts, while we will only contemplate them in perspective. They must come. It is impossible to look upon the map of North America, and not perceive the rationale of the project. Men may laugh at these suggestions; but when we are withdrawn from all the petty influences which now exist, these matters will assume the most grave and solemn national import.

I do not care to be in any way identified with them. They are the results of destiny, over which I have no control.

If the Treaty is not ratified, I will require all future negotiations to be transferred to Texas.

CHAPTER XIV:
Retirement—Houston's Character

Such was the destiny which, to the keen vision of Houston, awaited Texas if she remained a sovereign nation.

The extracts we have given from his dispatches put the question of his policy and his preferences, in regard to annexation, at rest forever. He was, up to the last moment, in favor of that great measure.

He favored it, because it would secure immediate peace to his fellow citizens, and protection from a perfidious and barbarous foe.

He favored it, because it would settle the affairs and establish the tranquility of the Republic, and enable him to withdraw from the turbulent scenes of political life, and enjoy the repose of retirement, after his long and ceaseless labors.

He favored it, because it would bind the people of Texas firmly to the great federal family of Washington, and link their fortunes to the American republic.

He favored it, because, like all the true and all the patriotic of his country, he felt an earnest longing to return to the family hearth-stone, where the great patriarchs of the Revolution had gathered, and unite with twenty millions of his brethren in burning incense to the Genius of Liberty around its holy altars.

He favored it, because he saw that it would narrow the field of many petty ambitious men, whose struggles for power might disturb the tranquility of Texas, and impede her advancement.

He favored it, because he felt he had himself achieved his work on the field and in the cabinet, and although he was beloved by the people, and could always have been, in one form or another, their leader, yet he had no more ambition to gratify. He believed, too, that his beloved country would find under our broad shield the same repose from her alarms and her troubles, that he himself looked forward to in the quiet of his

prairie home. And yet his dispatches show that he was prepared for any result. He had his eye fixed on the future, and if
American statesmen were resolved Texas never should mingle
her fortunes with us, he also was determined to watch over her
career and guide her to a nobler destiny.

Up to the very moment the decision was made by the American Senate, he held the question of annexation in the hollow
of his hand. And when, at the eleventh hour, we grudgingly
opened the doors to let the light of the single star shine into
our temple, there is not a shadow of doubt, that if Houston
had resented the tardy offer, it would have been, proudly and
scornfully hurled back by the people of Texas. He was not
then president, actually—but in or out of office he was still
their leader, the counselor of his country. His last term expired
just before annexation was passed, and the constitution would
not allow him to be president again. But his own confidential
friend, his Secretary of State, his adviser and his supporter,
was chosen to follow him, and it was everywhere understood
that Houston's policy was still followed—his feeling still consulted—and his voice still heard.

Great apprehensions were felt by the friends of Texas in this
country about the course Houston would finally pursue—for
it was believed that he would carry the people of that Republic with him in his decision. The time at last came,—Houston
gave his support to annexation, and by an overwhelming majority Texas became one of the sovereign states of the American republic.

Henceforth, for weal or woe, her fortunes were mingled with
the fortunes of the United States. Whether she will regret it,
is yet to be seen. She most certainly will rue the day she ever
sought refuge under our protection, unless she is allowed to
occupy a high and honorable place in our confederacy. She is
no outlaw, she is no menial—nor will she be treated as either.
With the richest soil and vast natural resources—with a wide
territory which stretches from the sea, where it blushes under

a tropical sun, to the north where it whitens with the eternal snow of the mountains—with a climate as balmy as the lands which are bathed by the blue waters of the Mediterranean—and, above all, with an ingenious, enterprising, and heroic people, she must become the garden of the New World. Let it be the pride of every man, whose inestimable privilege it is to say "I am an American Citizen," to extend towards Texas and the Texians his generous greeting. They have been misrepresented and traduced; but let us lift the odium from their name, for they *are* a brave and a magnanimous people, and let us be proud everywhere, whether it be by the firesides of our northern homes or in the courts of foreign princes, to call them brothers. Let us show to them and the world that the children of sires who bled at Bunker Hill and Yorktown, know how to prize the heroic men who rang out the Anglo-Saxon battle cry over the bloody field of San Jacinto.

But we are admonished that we have already trespassed far too long upon the patience of our kind readers. Our only excuse is, that, in tracing the fortunes of a brave people and their heroic leader, we have been beguiled by the pleasant lights and shadows that have fallen over the path where we were roaming. A few words, gentle reader, and we will abuse your goodness no longer—for we must not leave the hero of our humble story on the surges, as the elegant and philosophical Dumas did the noble Count of Monte Cristo. His predecessor had made war upon the Indians, and carried desolation to their peaceful wigwams. In their forest homes were heard the wailings of women whose chiefs had fallen by the hand of the white man; and the young Indian boy was sad because his chieftain father led him out no more on the warpath. Houston had seen injustice perpetrated upon the Red Men, and when his last term began, he at once sent the wampum among the forest tribes, and soon after went himself, in the Indian dress, to the distant woods and smoked the pipe of peace in the chieftains' dwellings. He made treaties with twenty-four different chiefs, and they regarded these treaties sacredly. Among them he felt safe—he wrapped his blanket about him, and laid himself down to sleep by the fires of ferocious savages, near whom other white men did not dare to venture. "We have nothing to fear from an Indian," he used to say, "if we only treat him with justice, and he believes us his friends." Peace was again restored along the frontiers, and the green corn was, again growing luxuriantly by the side of the primeval forests where the savage stealthily lurked for his game.

Houston paid off a large amount of debt incurred by his predecessor, due to other governments, arising from the prodigality of the administration. He created no new debt—administered the government on the basis of the revenues, and left the Exchequer Bills issued at the beginning of his term at par, with a considerable surplus in the treasury.

He left the country at peace with all the Indian tribes on the frontiers—the navy was laid up in port, for there was no use for it—the state was blessed with tranquility at home, the nation was prosperous—emigrants of the better class were rapidly pouring in from the north and from Europe; and the people were happy. The prisoners in Mexico were all restored to their homes—inland trade with Mexico was brisk and lucrative; — Texas was respected by all nations, and annexation was near its consummation.

Houston's last term expired. He could never be president again; and it was with no little sadness that the people saw him lay down the insignia of his office, and take leave of them, to return to private life. He was received back with joy by his family, and they thought that he would part from them no more. His home was on a rolling elevation in the midst of a green prairie, interspersed with islands of trees, and silver lakes, gleaming in the sunlight. His labors, his sorrows, and his struggles were over, and in the bosom of an affectionate family he expected to spend the last peaceful years of his stormy life in the noble pursuits of the husbandman.

Texas became one of the states of our confederacy, and she called her old leader from retirement once more, to represent her in the Senate at Washington. It is not strange that he yielded with deep reluctance—for he felt that in his quiet home he was as happy as the regards of the nation he had saved, the affection and society of his wife and his child, and the remembrance of sorrows past and victories won could make him. But he responded to the call of his country, and brought his republic and laid it on our federal altar.

CONCLUSION

"And so," said a friend to us a day or two ago, when we had read these few last pages, "you consider Houston a perfect character"—

No! far from it. In a world like ours, such a character probably does not exist: But we do believe, that it is filled with noble and generous hearts. The blight that has fallen on man has blotted out the fair image of perfection;—but it has not chilled every noble feeling—it has not annihilated heroism. And what higher office can we aspire to, than to seek for the noble, the magnanimous and the beautiful, and embalm it for coming times?

We know *all* of Houston's history. We know that his youth was wild and impetuous; but it was spotted by no crime, it was not even soiled by indulgence. His early manhood was filled with earnestness and daring, but it was deformed by no act which lost for him the confidence of the virtuous, or the doting love of his mother. We know, too, that just as he was stepping upon the theatre of high and brilliant fame, a cloud came over the sky, and wrapped his heart and his home in sadness and gloom.

There is a sorrow which even the hero cannot bear. The storms of life may beat against the frail dwelling of man as wildly as they will, and the proud and the generous heart may still withstand the blast. But when the poisoned shaft of disappointment strikes the bosom where *all* we love and live for is treasured, the fruit of this world turns to ashes, and the charm of life is broken. Then it is that too often reason and bliss take their flight together.

When this dark cloud fell over the path of Houston, he buried his sorrows in the flowing bowl. His indulgences began with the wreck of his hopes, and like many noble and generous spirits, he gave himself up to the fatal enchantress. But his excesses have been exaggerated by his enemies a hundred fold. We believe no man can say that he ever saw Houston rendered incompetent by any indulgences, to perform any of the offices of private or public life, a single hour.

But the days of his indulgences have long since passed away. When the sunlight of domestic happiness again shone through his dwelling, and he was sustained once more by that great conservative principle of a man's life—a happy home, illumined by the smile of an affectionate and devoted wife—his good angel came back again, and *for years no man has been more exemplary in all the duties and all the virtues of the citizen, the father and the husband.* From that moment he espoused the great cause of virtue and temperance, with all the earnestness of his nature.

Whenever an opportunity has been presented, he has eloquently spoken, in public and in private, in favor of that beneficent movement, which has restored many thousands of generous but misguided men to the long-abandoned embraces of weeping families, and to the noble duties of citizenship. And who could better tell the horrors and the woes of the poor inebriate's life than the man who had experienced them? Who could more eloquently and winningly woo back the wanderer to the fold of virtue, than he who had just returned to its hallowed enclosure? Blessings on the head of the devoted and beautiful wife, whose tender persuasions proved too strong for the clamors of appetite and the allurements of vice! In winning the stricken wanderer back to the pure charities of home, she saved the state one of its noblest citizens; and so benign has been the influence of his wonderful example, and so calm, and so holy a light beams ceaselessly around the altars of that distant prairie home, that his child will, with the nation he saved, rise up and call him blessed.

Houston's indulgences never were carried so far as to give a shock to his constitution. They were only occasional at any period. And now he finds himself standing on the meridian of life, with an erect, well-made form of perfect health and gigantic strength. His hair has been turned grey by Herculean labors, but his eye is still soft and clear, and it beams with a smile which no man can wear whose heart does not overflow with love of country and philanthropy to his race. His countenance is flushed with the glow of health and cheerfulness, which seldom, in a world like ours, lingers after the morning of life is passed. And but for occasional days of suffering from the wound he received in his right shoulder from two rifle-balls at To-ho-pe-ka, more than thirty years ago, he knows no physical ailment. Sometimes these sufferings are intense, and he will never be free from them while he lives, for no surgical skill has ever been able to close up that wound. It has discharged every day for more than thirty years. In a manner almost miraculous, he has entirely recovered from the wound in his ankle received at the battle of San Jacinto.

And thus we find ourselves at the close of our humble work. Would that some better pen had performed the task! But we could not forbear to make the offering, however unworthy it may be to history, to heroism, and to truth. And if it be an honor to human nature to repent, and abandon errors of opinion and frailties of conduct, why may not the biographer rejoice to weave the woof of such a story as Houston's, and throw it before the world, that all the wrong a great man may have inflict-

ed by the splendor of his talents—who had stooped to waste his time as Charles James Fox did, in garnishing vice by his genius, and ornamenting crime by its elevation, may be at last atoned for by the reformation of the admired individual transgressor! Such a case would seem to present one of the most captivating subjects in all history for the pen of a biographer.

IMPORTANT DISPATCHES & STATE PAPERS
ILLUSTRATIVE OF TEXAS HISTORY

OFFICIAL,
CITY OF HOUSTON,
April 16th, 1844.

GENTLEMEN:

Your notes have both reached me, one of the 30th ult., and one of the 1st inst. Today I forward to the State Department all my dispatches.

Col. Ashbel Smith, our Charge d' Affaires, writes from Paris, under date 29th February, this important fact. "The French and British Governments have united in a Protest to the United States against the annexation of Texas to the Union." This is an important fact. Never has the situation of Texas been so interesting since the 21st of April, 1836, as at this moment. You may rely upon it, if the Government of the United States does not act immediately, and consummate the work of annexation, Texas is for ever lost to them.

In my opinion, England and France will say to Texas, "if you will agree to remain separate for ever from the United States, we will forthwith prevent all farther molestation to you from Mexico, and guarantee you Independence, agreeably to your Institutions now established and avowed." You cannot fail to discover what would be the proper course of Texas in such an event. Texas has *done all* that she *could do*, to obtain annexation, and you may rely upon this fact, in the event of a failure, that Texas will *do all* that she *should do*.

If a Treaty is made, it will of course have been done after the pledges given by the United States Charge d' Affaires have been recognized by his government, and then we are secure.

If a Treaty has been made, and those pledges exacted by you, and it should be rejected, it will be proper to ascertain if annexation can take place by Congressional action, and this done promptly. Should all fail, you will forthwith call upon Mr. Packenham, the French Minister, as well as also the Government of the United States, and after suitable conversations and explanations, present to them the subject of a triple guarantee for our Independence, and to prevent all further molestation, or at least an unlimited truce with Mexico. And then if all prospect of annexation fails with the Government of the United States, and it should refuse to unite upon the basis here laid down, you will then, so far as practicable, arrange the matter with France and England, and General Henderson, with Mr. Miller, Secretary of the Secret Legation, will make a visit of leave to the heads of the proper departments, and return to Texas. Texas ought not, cannot, and will not remain in its present situation.

The subject of annexation has already embarrassed our relations with Mexico. The Truce will end on the first of May, as I presume, for I did not accede to the terms of the armistice, since Texas was recognized as a "Department of Mexico," in the terms of agreement between the commissioners. Mexico was well disposed to settle matters very amicably, when our commissioners arrived at Sabinus, but one of the Mexican commissioners was too unwell to proceed to business. When he recovered, the subject of annexation was mooted in the United States, and the Texian Congress, all of which had reached Mexico. Of these facts, in part, Gen. Henderson was apprised, and the anticipated rupture of our negotiations with Mexico was one reason why I was so careful to require of Gen. Murphy (endorsed by his Government), such pledges as would secure us against all contingencies that might arise to us, in consequence of our opening negotiations with the United States, on the subject of annexation.

This Government has been called on, and requested by her Majesty's Government, to state our relation to the Government of the United States. It was due to England, and her Majesty's Government was informed that an agent, Gen. Henderson, had been sent to Washington City, to negotiate upon the subject of annexation; but the particulars were not rendered. Since this occurred, I had an interview with Capt. Elliot, and I do not think the British Government will withdraw its friendly offices from the subject of Peace between Texas and Mexico.

It is reported here, that the Government of the United States has refused to sanction the pledges given by General Murphy. This surely cannot be the case. If so, you will have found yourselves in a most awkward dilemma. What—disavow such pledges when they were based upon Mr. Upshur's letter? I cannot believe this, unless the United States desired Texas to surrender herself to the uncertainty, or chances of annexation, contingent upon the various political influences which might interpose to the consummation of the object, and subject us to the injurious and annoying action of Mexico, instigated by the adhesion of Texas to the United States. A refusal on the part of that Government to secure us against consequences, which it has produced by *direct solicitation* of us, would be selfish in the extreme, and indeed I cannot conceive appropriate terms in which to characterize such conduct and policy, in an official dispatch. It would amount to this only—that if anything could be made out of Texas, by the United States, they were prepared and willing to derive the advantage, and if that could not be done, they wished to incur no responsibility on the account of Texas, but leave her to all the consequences which might possibly result to her from the course, which her generosity and credulity might induce her to pursue. Pitiable would our situation be if we were not annexed, and had required no pledges; fortunately, *this is not* our situation.

You have now all the grounds before you, and I hope you will ponder wisely and proceed securely for our safety.

It is palpable scandal to the 19th century, that Statesmen should be prating about the emancipation of persons born, and their race held in slavery, by the custom and consent of nations for centuries, while they permit Santa Anna to forge, and rivet chains upon eight millions of people who were born free. Thus will the horrors of slavery be increased, with design to render his success subservient to the subversion of the liberties of Texas, and form a new era in the history by degrading to slavery a portion of the Anglo-Saxon race. This ought not, and cannot be. It argues on the part of Statesmen a want of perception, as well as self-respect.

Gentlemen, you will keep the Government advised by every mail; and daily, of important events as they transpire. If you should be thrown for future reliance upon the friendly offices of Great Britain and France, you will, if possible, ascertain from them if they will act promptly, and what conditions they will expect of this Government.

Mr. Van Zandt has written that the United States were not willing to form any alliance with Texas, as it was contrary to their policy. Hence the necessity, upon the failure of the immediate annexation of this country to the confederacy of the North, and you will, as I have indicated, approach the Governments of England and France.

It is the first duty of statesmen and patriots to insure the liberty and well-being of their country. This is now our attitude, and every honest man in Texas will justify and approve that policy, which will place us in a situation where our liberties are secured, whether it be by annexation, or the establishment of our Independence. France and England will act effectively, if we do not permit ourselves to be trifled with and duped by the United States. But of this subject, as your situation may soon call your attention to it, you will be the best judges.

* * * * * * * * * * * *

This letter does not cancel former instructions from the Department; but it is designed to meet emergencies which may arise, or remedy those which have already arisen. Having awaited the arrival of your dispatches, and there being no time to forward them, and send a reply from the State Department, I have deemed it proper to write to you directly by the return mail; so that you may be ready, in the event of necessity, to take such action as our situation may require, and be prepared for contingencies.

> I have the honor to be,
> Your obt. servant,
> SAM HOUSTON

To GEN. J. P. HENDERSON
      and
HON. ISAAC VAN ZANDT
   &C. &C. &C

EXECUTIVE DEPARTMENT
Washington, July 29th, 1844

To His Excellency,
GENERAL ANTONIO LOPEZ DE SANTA ANNA,
President of the Republic of Mexico:

It appears by a letter received from General Adrian Woll, under date of the 19th ultimo, that you have entertained a desire to communicate with this government. I regret, however, extremely, that in so doing, you should have indulged in a departure from the courtesy which ordinarily obtains in the correspondence between civilized States of the present age. There are certain designated and universally acknowledged channels of intercourse between nations, such as the Department of State, or Foreign Affairs.

Through your subaltern, General Woll, you have, in the communication to which I allude, addressed no government, or functionary of any government. It is, however, addressed to Texians; but in language which even common courtesy does not sanction.

For the information of your Excellency, I will suggest, that the Commission sent out by this Government for the purpose of regulating the conditions of an Armistice between the two countries was authorized by the President of Texas, and as such must have been communicated to your Excellency; otherwise they could not have been received in their official capacity. Their credentials alone entitled them to the recognition of yourself or officers.

The Texian Commissioners had special and prescribed powers delegated to them, and all their acts were subject to the review and rejection, or approval of the Executive. Without approval, they could acquire no validity. The designation of Texas as a Department of the Mexican confederacy *so-called*, was highly obnoxious to the President, and consequently the conduct of the Commissioners was, at once, disapproved. For this, you are, now, Sir, pleased to express, through your subaltern, your *indignation* at the *perfidious* conduct of the people of Texas.

I regret much that you have given this complexion to the affairs of the two countries. When men, by chance or Providence, have been elevated to the rule of nations, and entrusted with the protection of the best interests of the people, it must be considered a great misfortune if they entail upon them calamities which their duties as philanthropists should teach them to avert.

When belligerents, even in the most angry excitement of feeling, are arrayed against each other, it is but proper that their chieftains should preserve toward each other that comity which might render them approachable, and thereby avert great human suffering and the effusion of human blood. When war rages, all ranks and conditions are subject to its agitations and calamities. Texas has already endured the extremest agony, and will endeavor to profit by her experience. Against her, you have again denounced war. We will await the event. Eight years ago, you were a suppliant; obtained your liberation without ransom, and acknowledged the Government of Texas. If Texas existed then as a nation, her recognition since then by other powers, and her increased commercial relations, would well excuse your recognition now of her sovereignty. But, Sir, you speak of your resources and power. They were defied and triumphed over in 1836; and if you invade Texas in 1844, you will find neither her prowess nor the success of her arms less complete.

I desire to know for what reason you have charged the authorities of Texas with perfidy. Have they given to Mexico any pledge they have not redeemed? They have liberated her chiefs and soldiers taken on the field of battle, without obligation so to do. But they are of a race which permit neither their word nor their honor to be falsified. How has it been with Mexico? The capitulation of Fannin was disregarded, and hundreds massacred in cold blood. You indeed denied a cognisance of this fact; declared that you were implicated by the falsehood of Gen. Urrea, and that if you ever returned to your country and came into power, you would execute him for his duplicity. Have you done it? You have power, but to what purpose? Of the inoffensive

Traders who visited Santa Fe, and capitulated to your officers, what was the treatment?

They were slaughtered by the way-side, when unable to march, and their ears cut off; evidences, indeed, of barbarity not heard of among nations pretending to be civilized, since the ninth century of the Christian era. Again, at the surrender of Mier, your officers pledged to the men the protection due to prisoners of war; in fulfillment of which, they were soon after barbarously decimated, and the remainder ever since held in chains and prison. They were also to be returned to their home immediately after their submission;—but every pledge given to them has been violated. Is this good faith? You pledged yourself also solemnly, through H. B. M. Ministers, to release the Texian prisoners in Mexico, if those of Mexico remaining in Texas, should be set at liberty—which was done on the part of this Government, by public proclamation, and safe conduct offered to them to return to their country. Have you performed your part of the agreement and your duty? Are they free? Will all this justify you in charging, through General Woll, either the Government or citizens of Texas with perfidy, or its Executive with double dealing in diplomacy?

I regret, Sir, extremely, that it bas been my duty thus to advert to circumstances which must be as disagreeable to you as to myself. But you have invoked it.

You have denounced war, and intend to prosecute it; do it presently. We will abide the result. Present yourself with a force that indicates a desire of conquest, and with all the appendages of your power, and I may respect your effort. But the marauding incursions which have heretofore characterized your molestation, will only deserve the contempt of honorable minds.

I have the honor, &c., &c.
SAM HOUSTON.

SENATE CHAMBER,
December 9th, 1844.

To His Excellency,
SAM HOUSTON, *President.*

I have the honor to transmit to your Excellency the following Resolutions, introduced by the Hon. David S. Kaufman, Senator from the District of Shelby, Sabine, and Harrison, and passed by the Senate.

1st. Resolved by the Senate, That the Administration of President Houston, which this day terminates, has been characterized by a forecast, economy, and ability, which entitle it to the thanks and gratitude of the Nation.

2d. Resolved, That as the Constitutional advisers of the President, we have undiminished confidence in the unbending integrity and devoted patriotism of Gen. Sam Houston, and he carries with him into retirement, our warm wishes for his health and happiness.

3d. Resolved, That the Secretary furnish Gen. Houston with a copy of these Resolutions.

With great respect,
HENRY J. JENET,
Secretary of the Senate

THE EAGLES OVER THE FIELD
OF SAN JACINTO

The flight of ravens through the dusky air,
The superstitious Roman deem'd
Propitious omen of triumphant arms.
And march'd to conquest—this his sole intent.
Empire along, his proud ambition fill'd;
For this he fought, and fame of daring deeds.
Empire was his, and fame of Heroism—
But warring to enslave—to ashes fell
The gilded, coreless fruit, unblest of Heaven.
Dark as the raven's wing, the breath of Fate
Swept o'er his conquests, and his empire fell
Albeit, his valor, with the empire, gained
And saved the mind's achievements—
Arts and sciences of nations conquer'd.
And last of all, amidst his trophies, shone
The two great lights of earth's Redemption:
The flame of Sinai, and Bethlehem's star;—
And yet he knew them not from darkness.

The Gothic Hero from his icy home
Came down and search'd them from the Seven Hills.
Thenceforth the vital germ of Freedom sprang.
The Saxon bore it to the Briton's home,
And he transplanted it in this New World.

Lo! what a glorious, soul-inspiring show
The tramp of Freedom through the Western World!
Look through the lens of Time, that gathers in
His mighty movements through the country—
How like a wonder, swells his vast procession;

From one small vessel's crew, to millions!
How rays his torch across the Continent;—
At every gleam an Empire springs to life—
At every gleam, a Despot's throne doth quake—
At every gleam through dark barbarians's wilds,
A State springs up, and golden harvests wave.
　　　　Stay not his course!—
See! on the western ocean's peaceful shore
His torch bright glowing, and his flag unfurled.
A dark spot intervenes—but all around,
The rays of civilization penetrate
Inevitably, to illumine all!
　　　　Fair Freedom's torch
Is blazing on the broad Pacific's shore,
That way from San Jacinto's battle-field
Flew—not the ominous Ravens of old Rome,
The talisman alone of victory and empire;—
The flight of Eagles told the Hero more—
Of Freedom's triumph o'er the Western World!

Look through the lens *again*, the future see;—
See Freedom's flag of interwoven dyes,
And torch of golden light, in every wave
Reflected.—Against the shores of Asia
See them dash illum'd all with hope-beams!
Against *all* shores they dash, diffusing light
Like young Auroras, o'er the world new-born.
Stay not their course!—Thou can'st not, if thou would'st.

** *These beautiful lines are furnished by a friend.*

www.ingramcontent.com/pod-product-compliance
Lightning Source LLC
Chambersburg PA
CBHW020337100426
42812CB00029B/3164/J